GREAT SPEECHES *for* BETTER SPEAKING

GREAT SPEECHES

for BETTER

SPEAKING

LISTEN AND LEARN FROM HISTORY'S MOST MEMORABLE SPEECHES

Michael E. Eidenmuller, Ph.D., AmericanRhetoric.com

New York   Chicago   San Francisco   Lisbon   London   Madrid   Mexico City
Milan   New Delhi   San Juan   Seoul   Singapore   Sydney   Toronto

1 2 3 4 5 6 7 8 9 10 11 12 13 14 15 16 17 18 19 20 21 22   DOC/DOC   0 9 8

ISBN 978-0-07-147229-6 (book and CDs)
MHID   0-07-147229-0 (book and CDs)

ISBN 978-0-07-147230-2 (book alone)
MHID   0-07-147230-4 (book alone)

Library of Congress Control Number: 2007941312

McGraw-Hill books are available at special quantity discounts to use as premiums and sales promotions or for use in corporate training programs. To contact a representative, please visit the Contact Us pages at www.mhprofessional.com.

Acknowledgments
Edward M. Kennedy's speech is used by permission of Liberty University.
Douglas MacArthur's speech is printed by permission of the General Douglas MacArthur Foundation, Norfolk, VA.
Mary Fisher's speech is printed by permission. Copyright © by the Mary Fisher Clinical AIDS Research and Education (CARE) Fund, University of Alabama–Birmingham.

This book is printed on acid-free paper.

*To my grandmother, whose passion for lifelong learning
in service to the collective good has provided a standard
by which the value of my life will be measured.*

*To my mother, who raised three relatively well-adjusted
men while successfully managing the demands of a notable
professional life, proving that such achievement is possible—
indeed, even likely—if you're strong enough.*

Contents

—4—

Structure 63

*Douglas MacArthur's Thayer Award
Acceptance Address*

—5—

Style 85

John F. Kennedy's Inaugural Address

—6—

Delivery 109

*Barbara Jordan's Statement on
the Articles of Impeachment*

—7—

Special Rhetorical Tactics 127

Mary Fisher's 1992 Republican National Convention Address

—8—

Great Speechmaking 153

§

Appendix: Speech Transcripts in Their Entirety 163

Glossary 203

References 207

Acknowledgments

I AM INDEBTED to Laurie Austin at the John F. Kennedy Library; Mary Fisher Productions Inc.; Colonel William J. Davis, Executive Director, the Douglas MacArthur Foundation; Liberty University; and the Ronald Reagan Presidential Library for granting copyright permission and providing audio versions of the speeches contained in this project.

Special thanks to my research assistants Kristle Bryan and Stacey Alexander for their diligent work in compiling and editing the background materials used in this project.

Thanks also to my colleagues at the University of Texas at Tyler for their encouragement and support during the writing of this book.

Finally, I am grateful to Holly McGuire, my sponsoring editor, and Julia Anderson Bauer, my project editor, with whose wisdom, patience, and grace this book was made possible.

GREAT
SPEECHES
for BETTER
SPEAKING

Introduction

───────── ❧ ❦ ─────────

WE HAVE GROWN suspicious of public oratory. During an age in which words can seemingly mean almost anything (and, therefore, almost nothing), public speechmaking is all too easily shamed. Weaned on the industrial-strength cynicism of programs such as "Saturday Night Live," "The Simpsons," and Comedy Central's "Daily Show" and "The Colbert Report," we get more pleasure from cleverly crafted ridicule than from honest, yet artful, eloquence. Moreover, by contemporary standards of comfort and attention, the sheer length of many our nation's finest historical speeches climbs well above the maximum allowable word limit of human tolerance. And so we have come to parade our rhetorical deficiencies under a banner of rhetorical suspicion.

These things were not always so. The speeches compiled in this book are reminders of a time when great American rhetoric well served that most fundamental and happy paradox of our way of life: Great speaking matters because democracy cannot just be practiced. It must also be preached. Despite our suspicions, we cannot have one without the other, for our best words invite our best deeds and together give us our best hope for securing the common good.

And yet, in almost open defiance of our lesser selves, a single speech, eloquently styled and forcefully delivered at a critical moment in time, still carries near-mystical power to transform everything. It happened on September 20, 2001, when the President of the United States delivered an address that gave desperately needed meaning to an almost incomprehensible tragedy, consoling our bereaved, inspiring our collective will, and commanding our national allegiance. It happened yet again from seemingly out of nowhere when a forty-three-year-old African-American from the land of Lincoln struck an astonishingly powerful keynote at the 2004 Democratic National Convention. In telling his own story, Barack Obama retold our national story and inspired us anew to rediscover that audacious hope that is our national birthright—the only lasting antidote to cynicism.

If this sounds a bit pedantic, I plead guilty. It is the special pleading of a professor of speech communication who counts it among the most gratifying experiences of his professional life to see young, apprehensive students of speech fundamentals turn into confident, experienced practitioners of public oratory. Admittedly, I sometimes go too far. For instance, I'd like to see public reviews of public rhetoric run closer to our characterizations of, say, Hollywood movies. "Exhilarating." "Sizzling." "Gripping." "Soaring." "Mesmerizing." "Giddy with energy." Theatrical descriptions like these might spark genuine curiosity and inspire us to look anew into the ancient and venerable craft of public speechmaking. Taking the cause further, emboldened reviewers might be motivated to move to a level of hyperbole commensurate with the best of Hollywood's offerings:

"Deeply engaging . . . moves the heart with sustained passion and the mind with unrivaled clarity . . . the gold standard for years to come."

" . . . rises to a level of sublime integrity that even a jaded intern would be well tempted to applaud."

"Everything else sounds like tedious filibustering."

"The delivery alone is worth two consecutive terms."

"Reports of great oratory's death have been greatly exaggerated."

"So, OK, professor, you're implying that our country fails to negotiate its 'happy paradox' because our leaders don't produce great oratory?" Brilliant! Well, sort of. Before we get to that admittedly tenuous proposition, we should probably first come to an understanding of what counts as "great oratory." That consideration is precisely where this book begins. What is "great oratory"? How do we recognized it? And in recognizing it, what can we thoughtfully say and do about it?

To address these questions, this book is organized topically. Chapters 2–7 identify a generic category of public speaking—a category germane to any given public speech, regardless of circumstance. The five categories are, in order of appearance: *situation, content, structure, style,* and *delivery.* Whatever else may be said of them, public speeches are necessarily given at a particular time and place, for a particular purpose, in front of a particular audience or set of audiences, by a speaker (situation). They contain a number of ideas and arguments (content) arranged in a particular order (structure), having peculiar properties of language (style) conveyed via the human voice (delivery).

For each category, a representative speech was selected as a model. The speeches in this book were chosen according to a few criteria. First and foremost, they were chosen for their overall merit. All of the speeches in this book enjoy widespread recognition for their significance in American history as well as for their eloquence and effectiveness in accomplishing the speaker's rhetorical goals. One authoritative example of this recognition is found in a study conducted by two distinguished scholars of speech communication, Stephen E. Lucas of the University of Wisconsin–Madison and Martin J. Medhurst of Baylor University, who surveyed more than a hundred professional critics of speechmaking and thereafter produced a list of the 100 greatest speeches of the twentieth century. All six of this book's speeches appear on that list. Two are in the top ten; four are in the top twenty.

Diversity was also a factor in speech selection. The speeches here are political and ceremonial in nature with contexts ranging from presidential impeachment hearings to national disasters to presidential inaugural addresses. The context of one speech forces us to consider whether it is possible for politics and religion to sit at the same public table, let alone break bread together. Two speeches were delivered by women, one an African-American. Casting an even wider diversity net, while desired, proved difficult in light of a third criterion involving the often murky and burdensome world of copyright law. The speeches chosen for this book are either in the public domain or permission rights were secured with relative ease, owing to the good graces of the copyright holders. While excerpts of the speeches appear in chapter text, the Appendix contains each speech in its entirety.

Chapter 1 sketches the fundamental philosophical ideas that surrounded the dramatic rise of populist persuasion in ancient Greece. The cause both for and against the nature and practice of rhetoric—the art of public speaking—was taken up by none other than Plato and Aristotle, two of Western culture's most influential thinkers. That debate and the critical issues it involved continue to provide much fodder for discussing the state of public oratory in our present day. Ultimately, you—the reader—will have to decide whether the judgments of Plato or Aristotle bear the most telling testament to the glories and trappings of public oratory in the United States.

Chapter 2 identifies the importance of the rhetorical situation using Ronald Reagan's space shuttle *Challenger* tragedy address as a model. Some political speeches arise from a complex set of circumstances that coalesce into a real or perceived crisis, one whose psychological, spiritual, political, and material implications are so devastating, or at least potentially devastating, that someone must say something about it—now! As we will see and hear, great oratories in these circumstances do three primary things for us: (1) they tell us what sense to make of the crisis; (2) they suggest how we should feel about the crisis and why; and (3) they prepare us to pursue a course of action.

The role that ideas and arguments—content—play in effective speechmaking is explored by analyzing Edward Kennedy's address to Liberty Baptist College in Chapter 3. An icon of the northeastern liberal political establishment's visit to an iconic institution of the evangelical Christian Right to deliver a speech on faith and truth is not only big news, it is a lesson. Kennedy's choice to address his evangelical audience on their own terms using biblical scripture, religious history, and constitutional interpretation, among other content strategies, to secure goodwill levels the ideological playing field and disarms his audience. For leaders facing similar situations, Kennedy's address is an exemplar of how the content of a speech can build bridges across divergent political interests and religious convictions to create a shared unity of purpose where none was apparent.

Chapter 4 describes the way in which the structure, or arrangement, of a speech can sustain audience attention as modeled by General Douglas MacArthur's Thayer Award address. Noteworthy is the way in which MacArthur uses a progression of ideas calculated to strike different shades or tones of emotion in his audience, thereby increasing the likelihood of sustained attention and retention of the speech content. Long known for an unwavering self-assuredness and a theatricality that some critics considered unseemly, MacArthur, in speaking for the one thing that mattered to him most—"the Corps"—crafted a masterpiece of ceremonial rhetoric in what was perhaps not merely the general's finest oratorical hour but quite probably the finest piece of military ceremonial rhetoric produced on American soil since Gettysburg.

The topic of language style, namely its character and role in adorning or "dressing up" the content of a speech, is explored in Chapter 5, with John F. Kennedy's heralded inaugural address as our model. By language style, I mean in particular those "figures of expression" in which the content of a speech is adorned, or dressed. Presidential inaugural ceremonies are very formal affairs, and the main attraction of these ceremonies, the inaugural address, must be styled accordingly to suit the occasion. It is important to remember that all speeches have a certain style. The style may be formal or informal, gracious or combative, alluring or dull.

Certain things must be said and styled in the same way. For example, expect "God" in some linguistic form to make an appearance, not as a matter of religious conviction so much as a kind of "rubber stamp," or perhaps less crudely styled, an "official seal" marking the solemnity of the occasion. Expect the themes of continuity and change to be styled in a way that countenances both Democratic and Republican interests in a mutually cooperative relationship—a striking counterbalance to the often contentious styling of presidential campaign speeches. John Kennedy, as we shall see, was particularly fond of brevity and clarity, which probably accounts for his copious use of *parallelism* and *antithesis*. (Parallelism uses successive words, phrases, or clauses with the same or very similar grammatical structure: "We shall *pay any price, bear any burden, meet any hardship, support any friend, oppose any foe* to assure the survival and the success of liberty." Antithesis is a contrasting of opposing ideas in adjacent phrases, clauses, or sentences: "That's one *small step for [a] man*; one *giant leap for mankind*.")

Both figures are calculated to convey precisely and only what needs to be said with the least amount of lexical effort. Kennedy was also fond of creating mental pictures with colorful metaphors. And if it is true that a picture is worth a thousand words, in public speaking it is equally true that "pictures" must be conveyed with words, and in Kennedy's style, the fewer words, the better.

There was one particular figure of expression that, as with fine china, Kennedy reserved for only the most important of rhetorical situations and, even then, for those rarified moments in the content where only a sublime level of eloquence would do. If you have any experience with Kennedy's inaugural you probably already know its most famous line. In reading the chapter on style, you will come to understand the particular figure of expression through which that line gets its stylistic force.

Chapter 6 discusses the use and manipulation of the human voice to deliver the content of a speech. Barbara Jordan's address to the Judiciary Committee of the U.S. House of Representatives and the American people during the Nixon impeachment hearings is the model here. Spoiler mini-warning! If you have never heard the voice of Barbara Jordan, you have a very big choice to make before listening to it. I could give you a clue as to what the voice of Barbara Jordan sounds like by saying that she was an African-American woman from Houston, Texas, but the clue would be misleading at best. The truth of the matter is there simply isn't any single speaker or speaking voice of which I am aware to which Jordan's voice can be helpfully compared. Superlatives about her voice abound, "God-like" and "thundering" to name just two. This is your choice: Listen first and then come back and read how and why her voice got that way. Or read first and see whether all the vocal pieces fit together the way you imagined as you listen to Jordan's speech. There are other options, of course. You could try to read and listen simultaneously or you could ping-pong back and forth, but I really don't recommend these to you. In any case, the choice you make now will significantly mediate your experience of the speech, so choose wisely.

Finally, Chapter 7 offers Mary Fisher's 1992 Republican National Convention address, a "Whisper of AIDS," to model various rhetorical tactics not explicitly covered in the previous chapters. Two terrifying Greek monsters, HIV/AIDS, and the most tendentious Republican National Convention in recent memory form the context of Fisher's address. In the end, as this speech shows, the rhetorical effectiveness of a speech hinges not only on a sound assessment of the rhetorical situation and a careful crafting of content, structure, style, and delivery. Sometimes "special rhetorical tactics" are required when multiple audiences and irksome cross-purposes come into play, as they did on that historic August 1992 evening in Houston, Texas. We will see these elements again in future national political conventions.

With all of that said, I have an admission to make. Treating a given speech within a single category alone proved too great a temptation at times for the simple reason that all of the chosen speeches are exemplary in more than one category. Douglas MacArthur's address at West Point contains moments of stylistic eloquence that rival those of Kennedy's inaugural address and in a few places even exceed them. Certainly, Kennedy's inaugural address is a model of linguistic eloquence. But consider these lines from MacArthur:

> *I do not know the dignity of their birth, but I do know the glory of their death. They died unquestioning, uncomplaining, with faith in their hearts, and on their lips the hope that we would go on to victory. Always, for them: Duty, Honor, Country; always their blood and sweat and tears, as we sought the way and the light and the truth.*

As this moment suggests, MacArthur's Thayer Award address is an exemplary model of style as well as structure. In more than a few places in MacArthur's address and in most every chapter I will have occasion to point out notable elements of a given speech beyond its designated category.

Consider another example. Barbara Jordan cultivated a thundering delivery that some maintain has been scientifically proven to scare the bark out of the meanest dog, or for that matter, off the toughest tree. But few are those who would be entirely disarmed by the stately certitude of Reagan's delivery in his *Challenger* address. So, I hope you'll forgive me if from time to time I address certain aspects of a given speech that move beyond the scope of its assigned category.

One other admission. This book offers a basic view of public speechmaking. It covers no new theoretical ground in the field of speech communication and is not intended to make a significant contribution to scholarship in that area. On that score, I am certain my colleagues will agree it is a resounding success. There is no shortage of serviceable works, some exceptional and a few truly seminal, that treat the subject of American rhetoric—its theory, analysis, criticism, and practice—with sustained intellectual depth and analytic rigor. This book is rather a modest attempt to treat the discipline and practice of public oratory in a light accessible to the general reader. It is much less a manual on how to speak effectively than it is a celebration of accomplished speakers who have delivered truly exceptional speeches. It is my hope that their examples will inspire a newfound appreciation for the role that great oratory has in American life.

A final note about this book's accompanying audio CDs. Each speech here is represented in its entirety. This is somewhat unusual for projects of this kind that typically provide only portions of a given speech. In addition, the effort was made to locate the highest quality audio artifact available and then to digitally enhance that audio. The result of these efforts is a remarkable audio experience in its own right. Whatever you make of the contents of the book, you will not find a better collection of high quality audio speeches in their entirety in a book of similar intent and scope.

Now, onward in our journey to discovering the greatness of our nation's best oratory.

1

The Great Debate

THE STORY OF oratory's place in the United States has its roots in ancient Greece and later in Rome where democratic values and institutions flourished. In these societies, open public debate and freedom of thought were integral to the maintenance of economic, political, military, and social infrastructures and attendant positions of leadership and power. Public speaking as a legitimate art or craft, as something to be studied, mastered, and practiced in service to the collective public good, gains much of its initial conceptual force from Greek philosophers Plato and Aristotle, two of the most influential figures in the Western intellectual and cultural tradition.

Plato dramatized his convictions about public oratory, or *rhetoric*, in a written dialogue entitled *Gorgias*. The title refers to a Sicilian ambassador named Gorgias who had journeyed to the great Greek city of Athens to plead for military assistance on behalf of his fellow citizens who were facing imminent war from neighboring Syracuse. Gorgias had been chosen to represent Sicily not on the strength of his character or goodness per se, but on his acknowledged skills as a public debater and captivating public speaker. His singularly bombastic brand of public oratory took the city of Athens by storm, as throngs of Athenian citizens turned out to hear him speak at ceremonial events and other public gatherings. This kind of public celebrity was accorded to a very select few Athenians and was unheard of for foreigners, something roughly equivalent to, say, John F. Kennedy's popularity in West Germany during the height of the Cold War.

Gorgias's displays of oratorical prowess might well have been easily dismissed by the city's leading power brokers as harmless theater were it not for the fact that he began offering to train other Athenian citizens in his particular brand of public persuasion. The offer came at a time when Athens had warmed to ideals of representative democracy. Positions of influence and power, long acquired by means of elite association or by military conquest, had become subject to the will of the majority. The increasing popularity of public oratory could cause any number of individuals to have to compete for the same political positions by bringing their case directly to the masses. It was here that the importance of Gorgias's offer to train individuals in public speaking carried particular force. Those who won the favor of the masses through the power of public address could expect to hold positions of substantial political, military, and economic influence.

This was all very troubling to Plato, who was convinced that the ideal society was one in which the best and most educated people ruled. The rulers of Plato's society were to be "philosopher-kings," men of temperate disposition who pursued wisdom. They alone would be capable of rising above the passions and prejudices of "the people"—to whom Plato would refer from time to time as "the herd"—to do what was in the best interests of society. For Plato, Gorgias was a symbol of the self-serving nature of rhetoric and the very embodiment of all that was dangerous about its power. Populist public speakers like Gorgias were inimical to the interests of a great society, and it was this cause that Plato took up in *Gorgias*.

Plato's challenges against the nature and function of public speaking could hardly go unchecked. There was too much power and profit at stake for those whose societal status depended on teaching and practicing it. And while Gorgias was a mesmerizing orator, he lacked the intellectual gravitas needed to meet Plato in the arena of public debate, especially since Plato's philosophical sword was wielded primarily in the form of the written word and not in an oratorical forum. What was needed to most effectively counter Plato's argument was another philosopher of the first intellectual order, someone from within Plato's own philosophical ranks, indeed from within his own Academy, the university started by Plato and generally considered to be the first and most illustrious academic institution in the West.

And so it was that Aristotle, Plato's prized pupil, well versed in the Platonic brand of philosophy, took up the cause for public oratory. The arguments by Plato and Aristotle concerning the nature and role of rhetoric are what I refer to as "the Great Debate." The Great Debate was not an actual one-time event, but rather a sustained series of objections and refutations delivered over time and by means of the written rather than the spoken word.

The Case Against Rhetoric

The case for Plato's prosecution of rhetoric took the form of two fundamental charges, namely that rhetoric was an intellectually illegitimate craft, and that it was useless at best and dangerous at worst to the ideals of a just and good society. Plato's view of intellectual legitimacy was predicated on three criteria: (1) a craft had to have definable and distinct subject matter (2) whose theoretical principles could be articulated and mastered (3) in service to the public good. By such criteria, music, for instance, was a legitimate art involving the subject of organized sound and silence in time, whose principles of melody, harmony, rhythm, structure, meter, and so forth, could be articulated, mastered, and ultimately performed with real-world benefit to society. Rhetoric, in Plato's view, failed the test of each of these criteria.

In *Gorgias*, Plato pits two characters, Socrates and Gorgias, in dialogue against each other. Socrates wonders openly whether rhetoric has a definable subject matter. Gorgias responds by claiming that the subject matter of rhetoric is "communication," an answer quickly dismissed on the grounds that every legitimate subject involves communication at some level, so there is nothing unique about rhetoric. When Socrates inquires about the status and role of public speaking, Gorgias arrogantly avers that rhetoric is the master craft in that it holds all other crafts under its power. Thus, if a person who had mastered the art of medicine were to debate a master of rhetoric in front of the people on the issue of who between them would make a better surgeon general, the master of rhetoric would win hands down simply by great oratory's capacity for winning the favor of the crowd. Socrates concludes that if this is so, rhetoric is indeed a very dangerous thing since it has the power to give the appearance of expertise where none actually exists. Socrates goes on to assert that rhetoric is concerned chiefly with the appearance rather than the reality of truth or justice. Its real aim is power and shameful self-promotion, a power that is not gained through careful and disciplined study but by an acquired habit of and taste for flattering an audience. And since flattery has no definable principles of its own, rhetoric fails all three tests of artistic legitimacy.

The Case for Rhetoric

Aristotle's case for the defense of rhetoric is found in his treatise *On Rhetoric*. To the charge that rhetoric is an illegitimate craft, Aristotle responds that its subject matter is communication, but not merely in the sense of transmitting information. Rhetoric is a particular kind of *persuasive* communication that aims at influencing human belief and behavior. More than that, rhetoric is strategic persuasion carried out in courts of law (forensic rhetoric), at political assemblies (deliberative rhetoric), and at various ceremonial occasions such as at the Olympic Games and at funerals (epideictic rhetoric). Moreover, responds Aristotle, rhetoric does have theoretical principles readily identifiable in the categories of content (the appeal of the ideas, arguments, and messages), arrangement (the structure of that content), style (the particular kind of language and linguistic devices used to express that content), and delivery (the verbal and nonverbal means by which content is transmitted between speaker and audience). No other art or craft can claim the same definable subject matter with the same clearly articulated theoretical principles toward the collective public good as can the art of rhetoric.

Plato's second charge concerning the danger that artful public speaking poses to society is met with a strong response. Aristotle grants that oratory can be used for ignoble purposes and that its targeting of a mass of people who lack the requisite level of knowledge by which to make good and just decisions constitutes a clear and present danger to society. But surely the best response to this danger cannot be merely to rid ourselves of oratory altogether. Many important decisions pertaining to the health and maintenance of a society are predicated on the use of public speech to move audiences to conviction and action. Surely Plato isn't advocating that democracy itself, insofar as its working institutions and processes necessarily utilize public speaking to help citizens form the right opinions and make just decisions, be abandoned.

Rather, maintains Aristotle, we ought to preserve the integrity of our working democracy not by abandoning the pursuit of artful oratory but by training its citizens to learn its artful ways, so that all free citizens can use it for the collective good. Let us give the medical expert the same rhetorical advantage as the nonexpert. Let us give the prosecutor the same advantage as the defense attorney. Let truth and justice come to fruition when both sides avail themselves equally of the art of persuasion. Rhetoric, concludes Aristotle, is useful because it gives truth and justice a fighting chance in the real world of competing demands and interests germane to a vibrant democracy.

Aristotle further argues that, unlike Plato's relatively dull and burdensome philosophical method of inquiry, rhetoric's appeal to both the mind and the heart makes it the best way to educate the masses, who admittedly have little interest in or capacity for pursuing wisdom in the way of the philosophy. That is, great oratory is a useful vehicle by which to educate the people, even if it means gratifying their senses in order to do so. A sick person who would not take a bitter pill to get well will do so if that pill is surfaced in sweetness.

The art of rhetoric, according to Aristotle, is useful in teaching a person to examine all sides of an issue and thus not only provides a justification for considering multiple perspectives but serves also to prepare against the strategic attacks of an opponent. The craft of rhetoric provides a means of gauging the relative strength of your opponent's position so that you can better prepare your own.

Finally, observes Aristotle, if humans are in any important sense distinct from other animals, surely that mark of distinction lies in the power to adjudicate problems and tensions with other humans by way of strategic verbal entreaty rather than sheer physical violence. Rhetoric promotes peace—or at least offers the promise for its promotion—in that it holds out humankind's best hope for the art of words to rule over the art of war.

Implications of the Great Debate

The Great Debate is hardly over. While Plato and Aristotle have long since passed from the scene, the implications of their convictions concerning the nature and value of rhetoric are alive and well in Western culture today. For our purposes, we note that the Great Debate has given us a set of conceptual tools we can use to make sense of the world around us, a world that is very much both cause and effect, process and product of a rhetorical engagement whose roots cut deep into and across Western cultural traditions and their democratic systems and institutions of power.

In the speeches that follow, the mindful reader will see, hear, and feel the weight of Plato's charges and also of Aristotle's refutations on the question of great oratory's nature and function in our society.

I'll admit, insofar as the speeches in this book represent some of the best oratory yet produced on American soil, the case is weighted in favor of Aristotle. Ultimately, you must decide the great questions about oratory's place in American democracy. It is you, the citizen-reader of this text, who must sit in judgment and decide who wins the Great Debate, for its spirit and substance are very much alive in Western civilization and will remain so as long as democratic ideals of freedom and liberty remain the subject and practice of Western culture.

2

Situation

Ronald Reagan's Space Shuttle Challenger *Address*

ON JANUARY 28, 1986, the United States watched in horror as the space shuttle *Challenger* burst into flames shortly after takeoff. The single worst disaster in NASA's storied history in space at the time—tragically, the space shuttle *Columbia* would suffer a similar fate in 2003, disintegrating upon re-entry and killing all seven of its crew—prompted a speech that revived our hopes and dreams in the wonders of scientific discovery.

President Ronald Reagan, who had been preparing to deliver his State of the Union address that night, instead delivered a stirring speech to the nation addressing this national tragedy. This speech, lauded for many reasons, shows mastery of the rhetorical situation.

Ronald Wilson Reagan

Ronald Wilson Reagan (February 6, 1911–June 5, 2004) was born in Tampico, Illinois, to John and Nelle Reagan. The young Reagan displayed an interest in acting at an early age, performing in church skits and high school and college plays. After graduating from Eureka College, Reagan took a job as a radio announcer in Iowa, where he created a play-by-play broadcast, based upon telegraph reports alone, of Chicago Cubs baseball games.

Reagan moved to Hollywood after a successful screen test for Warner Brothers film studios. He would go on to appear in some fifty movies, including such notable roles as George Gipp in *Knute Rockne, All American* and a critically acclaimed portrayal of Drake McHugh in *Kings Row*. The experiences drawn from his comedic and dramatic roles would prove a useful resource for Reagan during his presidential years. Reagan himself understood the value that his acting experience brought to the presidency. Asked once if he thought it possible for an actor to be president, Reagan responded by asking how it could be possible for somebody to be president without being an actor.

Reagan's role in *Knute Rockne* is worth mentioning in relation to his *Challenger* address. Both "scripts" were based around a drama of epic proportions in which a hero, removed from the actual events themselves, is nevertheless called upon to preside over them. In both instances, Reagan was called upon to carry the day with an inspirational speech delivered in relatively subdued terms. Reagan learned to play a range of character roles that would help him carve out a populist appeal and could move comfortably and credibly between playful and poignant, tragic and heroic storytelling. The Reagan range would prove a powerful inducement for winning allegiances on both sides of the political fence.

If Reagan's acting skills were made by Hollywood, his public speaking chops were a product of corporate ingenuity honed on the road. During the 1950s, Reagan became a spokesman for General Electric. He was, by his own account, a "circuit speaker" for the company but he also found occasion to inject political rhetoric into his corporate speeches.

Reagan's rise in politics began in 1962. After being fired by GE, Reagan, a career "New Deal" Democrat, switched parties, saying he was dissatisfied with the "big government" direction that the Democrats had taken. In 1964, Reagan vaulted onto the national political stage with a taped television address supporting the candidacy of the Republican Party's presidential nominee, Barry Goldwater. Although Goldwater lost the election, national audiences were treated for the first time to Reagan's populist conservatism. Reagan was elected governor of California in 1966, serving two terms through 1974. In 1980, Reagan was elected the fortieth U.S. president and was elected to a second consecutive term in office in a landslide victory over Democratic presidential nominee Walter Mondale.

Owing to a nearly unprecedented populist appeal, Reagan came to be known as "the Great Communicator," a moniker that Reagan himself liked and that held dual connotations. For those whose politics agreed with Reagan's, he was a master at selling a conservative Republican agenda. For those whose political views differed from Reagan's, the label was a reminder of how the power of his persona could override. Even among his detractors, Reagan was a "likeable fellow." He could speak agreeably to all even if some despised what he said. The Reagan range would play an important role in how different audiences would come to understand the meaning and significance of the space shuttle *Challenger* disaster.

Theory of Situation

Public speeches do not arise in a vacuum of rhetorical possibility. Good public speeches are born of rhetorical opportunity. Great public speeches are born of rhetorical *necessity*. Namely, something has happened, is happening, or will soon happen that is so significant to some group of people that someone *must* say something about it—now. When the right combination of time, circumstance, and necessity falls into place, we have the makings of a genuine rhetorical situation.

A rhetorical situation is one in which a problem or crisis is capable of being redressed in whole or in part through the power of speech alone. A quick sketch of the features of a rhetorical situation includes a *problem* or crisis, a *purpose*, an *audience*, a *subject*, and, of course, a *speaker*. Not all situations are rhetorical. There may be a crisis, but no one to speak. There may be a speaker but no one to listen. There may be a crisis, a speaker, and an audience, but the power of speech alone can do nothing to ameliorate the situation. No amount of public speechmaking, however impassioned, would have prevented Hurricane Katrina from whipping her way across the Gulf Coast, destroying lives, and wreaking hundreds of millions of dollars worth of damage. Disasters, natural or man-made, cannot be undone by the power of speech alone. Public speeches cannot raise the dead.

However, catastrophic events do provide the basis for rhetorical situations. Despair, anxiety, fear, anger, and the loss of meaning and purpose are powerful psycho-spiritual forces that deeply affect us all. It has been said that "without hope the people perish." And without hearing powerful and timely words of encouragement, the people may never find cause for hope. In taking stock of a rhetorical problem or crisis, it is important to ask questions. What has actually happened? How serious is it? Who and whose interests are affected? These are questions that help us identify the scope of a problem or crisis.

The answers to these questions lead to the formulation of a rhetorical purpose. Broadly considered, rhetorical purposes target two main objectives: human belief and human action. Speeches attempt to create, influence, reinforce, undermine, and even destroy beliefs. In addition, public speeches may also motivate us to take or to refrain from taking some action. Rhetorical purposes are tidy two-part terms that express ways of accomplishing one or both of these objectives. Examples include "to educate," "to persuade," "to console," "to inspire," and "to motivate." A philosopher addressing a group of students about the passing of the industrial age and the advent of a new age of biotechnology may have as his purpose "to educate" with the objective of creating a new set of beliefs. Political campaign speeches alternatively attempt to undermine some beliefs—for example, about certain candidates and the platforms they represent—and to reinforce others. A preacher addressing a congregation on the divinity of Jesus is likely attempting to reinforce a set of beliefs.

Problems and purposes are important features of a rhetorical situation. We have yet to consider the remaining three: audience, subject, and speaker.

If there is one commandment that rises to near-biblical proportions in the art of public speaking it is this: "Know thy audience." Politicians, preachers, lawyers, and advertising and public relations agencies spend small fortunes in obedience to this commandment. Purveyors of public messages must take stock of what audiences know, believe, desire, and want, and they must use this information to formulate strategies to accomplish their rhetorical objectives. A speech designed to persuade middle-aged adults to quit smoking might be filled with medical trend statistics demonstrating the effects of smoking for ten to forty years and the benefits of quitting later in life. To convince an audience of young schoolchildren not to start smoking cigarettes, a speech may enlist quotations from teen icons to the effect that smoking isn't cool. It may include displaying graphic photos comparing normal lung tissue with tissue ravaged by a lifetime of smoking. In any case, target audiences must be clearly identified.

At first blush, subject seems a fairly straightforward feature of a rhetorical situation. What will be talked about? In the case of the speech in this chapter, the answer would simply be the space shuttle *Challenger* tragedy. But this gives rise to another question, What in particular about the tragedy will you discuss? Will you talk only about the crash itself? Will you include the history leading up to and including the tragedy? If so, how much and which part of history? Will you talk about the astronauts? The reasons behind the crash? The families of the victims and their stories? What about the role of the media in influencing perceptions of the crash? The scope, breadth, and depth of what is and is not covered must be painstakingly considered for every speech subject. If everything about a subject is potentially in play, then potentially nothing is. As you will see and hear, pinpointing the scope of the *Challenger* address was one of most critical considerations of the rhetorical situation, requiring careful planning and skill to achieve a few strategic objectives.

Finally, every rhetorical situation begins and ends with a speaker. The speaker in a rhetorical situation is the primary agent responsible for delivering the goods. He or she is charged with identifying the parameters of the problem, clarifying the scope of the subject, addressing the relevant audience or audiences, and accomplishing the rhetorical objectives. That's a lot of responsibility, rhetorically speaking.

With the concept of rhetorical situation and its five elements in mind, we are ready to put the space shuttle *Challenger* disaster in context. As with most all such situations, there is a story behind it. That story must be told first in order to appreciate how the elements of the *Challenger*'s rhetorical situation were artfully navigated to form one of the greatest speeches of its kind in American history.

The Tragedy

The launching of the space shuttle *Challenger* had been twice delayed. Its original launch date of January 22 was scrapped due to inclement weather. A second delay was technical in nature, a defective micro switch in the hatch-locking mechanism that caused problems removing the hatch handle. Adding to the obvious pressure NASA felt with each delay was the White House's insistence that the shuttle be in space by the time Reagan gave his State of the Union address, which had been scheduled for January 28. Education was an important agenda item for the address, and Reagan had planned to laud the *Challenger* as a shining example of scientific achievement born of America's science education.

Reagan planned to put a human face on that education by singling out one of the mission's crew, Christa McAuliffe, who was one of NASA's first civilians in space. McAuliffe, a social studies teacher at Concord High School in New Hampshire, was the beneficiary of NASA's Teacher in Space Program. The program's intent was largely a public relations effort designed to promote greater interest in the space program and to foster renewed support for science education in general. The mission was in this sense a real-time public service announcement. McAuliffe had impressed NASA officials as someone who could be painted as an ordinary person but also a gifted teacher. One of the mission's plans had even included real-time communication between McAuliffe and some students while the shuttle was in orbit.

At 11:38 A.M. (EST) on January 28, 1986, a bright and clear morning, the *Challenger* was cleared for takeoff. Aboard were Christa McAuliffe and six other crew members. Of the major networks, CNN provided the only live coverage of the shuttle's liftoff. Among those watching were many of the nation's schoolchildren. According to a *New York Times* poll, nearly 50 percent of schoolchildren aged nine to thirteen watched the event live in their classrooms.

At ignition (T+0), the space shuttle lifted off from its launch base near Cape Canaveral in Florida. Within seconds, a systems engineer from mission control in Houston confirmed liftoff—all systems go. At T+59 seconds, following a series of routine flight maneuvers, tracking cameras spotted a small fire on one of the fuel tanks. Seconds later a "large ball of orange fire" appeared on the side of the main fuel tank. This fire grew rapidly. At T+72 seconds, *Challenger* shuttle pilot Michael Smith said, "Uh, oh" over the radio. It was the last verbal transmission delivered from the vessel. To those watching on television it appeared that the *Challenger* had been enveloped in a fiery plume of thick, white smoke. Gradually, as the plume began to disperse, it became evident that the shuttle had disintegrated.

News of the disaster diffused rapidly through the major television networks, as broadcasters cut in to regularly scheduled programming to report on it. ABC's Peter Jennings, the first to broadcast, confessed his confusion on air: "We are in the dark as much as you are." Tom Brokaw of NBC wondered aloud if NASA had gone too far too soon by putting a schoolteacher on board the flight. CBS's Lesley Stahl reported later that President Reagan "couldn't get the schoolteacher off his mind." Television viewers wouldn't be able to either, as all three networks interspliced stock footage of McAuliffe with the shuttle's disintegration throughout the remainder of the day.

The *Challenger* tragedy now occupied front and center stage in the national consciousness, forcing Reagan to cancel his State of the Union address. Speechwriter Peggy Noonan, along with other presidential staff speechwriters, moved quickly to draft an appropriate response—to be delivered later that evening—to the crisis. A rhetorical situation was born. The nation was in a collective state of shock; schoolchildren were confused; families of the deceased were bereaved; NASA officials feared for their professional lives; and millions of Americans wondered what to make of it all.

In addressing the American people on an event of national scope, Reagan would play the role of national eulogist. In that role, he would need to imbue the event with life-affirming meaning, praise the deceased, and manage a gamut of emotions accompanying this unforeseen and yet unaccounted-for disaster. As national eulogist, Reagan would have to offer redemptive hope to his audiences, and particularly to those most directly affected by the disaster. But Reagan would have to be more than just a eulogist. He would also have to be a U.S. president, for the implications of the *Challenger* disaster touched upon important political issues that concerned America's allies and detractors, most especially the Soviet Union. And Reagan would have to carry it all with due presidential dignity befitting the office as well as the subject matter.

Ronald Reagan's Mastery of Situation

Ladies and Gentlemen, I'd planned to speak to you tonight to report on the state of the Union, but the events of earlier today have led me to change those plans. Today is a day for mourning and remembering. Nancy and I are pained to the core by the tragedy of the shuttle Challenger. *We know we share this pain with all of the people of our country. This is truly a national loss.*

Reagan begins his response to the rhetorical situation by marking the significance of the occasion. State of the Union addresses are annual speeches delivered to a joint session of Congress and now televised nationally. Narrowly concerned, the State of the Union address is a kind of national progress report noting the most important accomplishments of the executive and legislative branches of government during the previous year and including important prospects and challenges upcoming. More broadly, it is a constitutionally sanctioned performance of democracy, the one time each year when the people's representatives come together with the people to coparticipate in the nation's past, present, and future democratic glory. With so much planning done, and given its symbolic importance, it would take a very significant event to reschedule the State of the Union address, and Reagan marked the event accordingly.

Reagan begins the address by characterizing the tragedy in the most general of terms. The events that brought forth this rhetorical situation are still very fresh. By using a generic description in "events of earlier today," Reagan gently eases his audiences into the grim reality. Then he characterizes the events firmly but still gently as a "national loss." It is not only a loss for the family members and friends of the American astronauts. It most certainly is not only a loss for NASA. It is *our* loss, and we must feel it and understand it as such.

The rhetorical situation is still emotionally unstable, and the natural emotions of anger, shame, and fear that accompany a tragedy must be carefully managed. Reagan moves to direct these emotions. This is not the time for skeptical inquiry or the casting of stones. It is not a day for technical analysis. All things will happen in their due time. Now is the time for "mourning and remembering." Thus, the meaning of the event has been framed explicitly as a national eulogy with Reagan presiding as national

eulogist. In this way, Reagan positions himself both outside the fray as one presiding over it and as one inside of it
who shares its painful reality.

> *Nineteen years ago, almost to the day, we lost three*
> *astronauts in a terrible accident on the ground. But*
> *we've never lost an astronaut in flight. We've never*
> *had a tragedy like this. And perhaps we've forgotten*
> *the courage it took for the crew of the shuttle. But*
> *they, the* Challenger *Seven, were aware of the*
> *dangers, but overcame them and did their jobs*
> *brilliantly. We mourn seven heroes: Michael Smith,*
> *Dick Scobee, Judith Resnik, Ronald McNair, Ellison*
> *Onizuka, Gregory Jarvis, and Christa McAuliffe. We*
> *mourn their loss as a nation together.*

Moving forward, Reagan positions the tragedy within a
larger picture without losing the special significance of
the present tragedy. The allusion of "lost three astronauts"
refers to the *Apollo 1* spacecraft, which was destroyed during a training exercise on January 27, 1967, killing all three
astronauts on board. But the special significance of *Challenger* is kept in full view by naming each of the crew
members killed. Here also, Reagan praises the fallen crew
members by noting the "courage" of our "seven heroes."
To further manage our emotions and to continue directing
our thoughts on the event's meaning, Reagan again calls
us to national mourning.

> *For the families of the seven, we cannot bear, as you*
> *do, the full impact of this tragedy. But we feel the*
> *loss, and we're thinking about you so very much. Your*

loved ones were daring and brave, and they had that
special grace, that special spirit that says, "Give me a
challenge, and I'll meet it with joy." They had a hunger
to explore the universe and discover its truths. They
wished to serve, and they did. They served all of us.

With Reagan's primary audience constituted as collective
mourners, the next situational demand requires a parti-
tioning of the audience into respective interest groups or
sub-audiences. It is as though the camera, having panned
a wide angle shot of the entire audience to this point, now
narrows in to focus our sympathies on a particular section of the audience. The first sub-audience is the families
of the astronauts, those most personally affected by the
tragedy. Reagan's rhetoric here treads carefully so as not to
cross over into that sacred space that is the special province
of family units. He specifically acknowledges the inap-
propriateness of suggesting how they should feel. What
Reagan can and does do is offer a measure of praise that
each family member can personally take hold of. "Daring," "brave," "special grace," and "special spirit" are all
laudatory terms that family members can claim for their
own. With the line "They served us all," Reagan's "camera"
pans back and reestablishes the connection of the part to
the whole. The families have received due consolation and
a place of mourning and remembrance to call their own
but, through the dutiful service of the astronauts, are also
connected with the larger corporate body of mourners.

We've grown used to wonders in this century. It's hard
to dazzle us. But for twenty-five years the United
States space program has been doing just that. We've

grown used to the idea of space, and, perhaps we forget
that we've only just begun. We're still pioneers. They,
the members of the Challenger *crew, were pioneers.*

Reagan next momentarily draws our attention away from
individual audience interests to the larger scientific story in
which the space shuttle *Challenger* participates. Electrifica-
tion, the automobile, the airplane, radio, television, and
motion pictures, the telephone, air conditioning and refrig-
eration, nuclear fission, and, of course, space exploration
marked a series of twentieth-century scientific advances
unrivaled in scope and number in human history. NASA's
dazzling scientific achievements take their place among
these.

The big news of this section, however, is Reagan's use
of the word "pioneers" to characterize the *Challenger* crew.
Reagan envisions the *Challenger* crew's place in history as
transcending the scientific exploits of one century and the
realm of science altogether. "Pioneer" cloaks the astronauts
in a mythical covering, one dating back to our nation's ear-
liest ventures. Pioneers of the North American West faced
hardship, danger, and death. The term "pioneer" both connects the event to a mythic past and provides a logic by
which the death of the astronauts is fashioned as a reasonable outcome of their endeavors.

And I want to say something to the schoolchildren of
America who were watching the live coverage of the
shuttle's takeoff. I know it's hard to understand, but
sometimes painful things like this happen. It's all part
of the process of exploration and discovery. It's all part
of taking a chance and expanding man's horizons. The
future doesn't belong to the fainthearted; it belongs to

> *the brave. The* Challenger *crew was pulling us into
> the future, and we'll continue to follow them.*

Reagan's next sub-audience is the schoolchildren, an estimated five million, among them the students of Christa
McAuliffe's class and school. In saying, "I know it's hard
to understand, but sometimes painful things like this happen," Reagan momentarily adopts the tone of an empa-
thizing parent. This is a difficult tone to strike while also
remaining "presidential," but Reagan carries it well enough,
if only because it comes as a brief interlude. It is also a mod-
erately successful way to reach the children. The rhetorical
situation required Reagan to single out the schoolchildren
as a group, and although the choice not to specifically identify Christa McAuliffe's students is sound, the comfort that
the children might be expected to get in the statements that
follow is questionable. Young schoolchildren would likely
find it less than comforting to hear that death awaits those
who are "brave" enough to grow up.

> *I've always had great faith in and respect for our space
> program. And what happened today does nothing to
> diminish it. We don't hide our space program. We
> don't keep secrets and cover things up. We do it all up
> front and in public. That's the way freedom is, and we
> wouldn't change it for a minute.*

Here, Reagan the national eulogist hands off to Reagan
the U.S. president and leader of the free world. This passage contains the only patently political statement in
the address. The reference to hiding the space program
trades some of the shame associated with the tragedy with
the even greater shame of failing to come clean with the

truth. This is a direct attack on the secrecy with which the Soviet Union handled some of its space exploration activities. Although the Soviet space program could boast many firsts—first satellite, first animal to enter Earth's orbit, first probe launched to Mars and Venus, first woman in space, first permanently manned space station, among many others—the program's failure to report some of its fundamental failures, including cosmonaut fatalities and aborted launches, drew the ire of American scientists who knew that shared scientific knowledge was the best way to ensure the stability of scientific programs that relied on federal funding for their existence. Reagan would exploit this secrecy as a major difference between democratic and totalitarian political systems.

> *We'll continue our quest in space. There will be more shuttle flights and more shuttle crews and, yes, more volunteers, more civilians, more teachers in space. Nothing ends here; our hopes and our journeys continue.*
>
> *I want to add that I wish I could talk to every man and woman who works for NASA, or who worked on this mission and tell them: "Your dedication and professionalism have moved and impressed us for decades. And we know of your anguish. We share it."*

This direct address to NASA and its employees is Reagan's third foray into a particular subset of his audience. Less the national eulogist, Reagan presents his prospects for NASA's future with resounding presidential authority. Whereas Reagan has, up to this point, connected the event with our nation's proud history, here he signals our expectations for the future and with this gives needed encouragement to all those associated with NASA. Reagan ends this portion of the speech with "We share it," once again connecting the part to the whole.

> *The crew of the space shuttle* Challenger *honored us by the manner in which they lived their lives. We will never forget them, nor the last time we saw them, this morning, as they prepared for their journey and waved goodbye and "slipped the surly bonds of Earth" to "touch the face of God."*

In closing his address, Reagan adopts for the last time the posture of the national eulogist.

It is both an eloquent and poetic rhetorical moment. It is eloquent in that it captures the mythological sentiment surrounding humankind's unending quest to solve the mysteries of the unknown. Those unfamiliar with the history of exploration would likely interpret the final phrase "touch the face of God" as a kind of oratorical sacrament of "last rites," a final point of earthly contact before sending the eulogized to their final resting place. For those more acquainted with aviation history there is a special meaning in the final phrase. The quotation is taken from a poem entitled "High Flight" by the American aviator and poet John Magee who died fighting in World War II while serving in the Royal Canadian Air Force. The story goes that Magee, climbing ever higher in his Spitfire, was seized by the words "To touch the face of God." (The words "touched the face of God" also conclude a poem by Cuthbert Hicks entitled "The Blind Man Flies," which appeared in a 1938 anthology on flight poetry.)

The National Eulogist

Ronald Reagan's space shuttle *Challenger* address is a model of how great oratory manages the demands and requirements of a rhetorical situation. The speech succeeds in meeting the emotional requirements of its various audiences. Families of the deceased crew members, the nation's schoolchildren, and NASA and its employees, and benefactors were each met on their own emotional terms. But Reagan also took care to connect those audiences to the large constituted audience of American mourners. In the final analysis, Reagan's address brought together disparate groups by constituting them as a single organic whole, a nation of people called to a place of national mourning and remembering.

Reagan, as speaker, also managed the rhetorical situation by styling himself both as U.S. president and as national eulogist, trading roles appropriately as the interests of different audiences required. This ability to credibly move in and out of different roles for different audiences was a large part of what made Ronald Reagan the Great Communicator.

3

Content

Edward M. Kennedy's
"Faith and Country, Tolerance and
Truth in America"

A MISDIRECTED MEMBERSHIP solicitation created a unique meeting of the minds at Liberty Baptist College, now Liberty University, on October 3, 1983, when Senator Edward Kennedy addressed a potentially hostile audience with a masterful speech. Kennedy's use of content, as we will see in this chapter, had a great deal to do with the speech's success.

Edward Kennedy

Edward (Ted) Moore Kennedy (February 22, 1932–) was born in Brookline, Massachusetts, to a prominent Irish Catholic family, the youngest child of Joseph and Rose Kennedy. His father, a highly successful businessman and enigmatic political figure in his own right, was a former U.S. ambassador to Britain and longtime leader within the Democratic Party. His mother, Rose Kennedy, gave birth to nine children, including President John F. Kennedy and U.S. Attorney General Robert Kennedy. Active in various philanthropic pursuits, Rose Kennedy received the title of "papal countess" from the Vatican in recognition of her "exemplary motherhood and many charitable works." Politics and religion, if not always abiding hand in glove, were never far removed from each other for the Kennedy family.

Along with older brothers John and Robert—and to a lesser extent eldest brother Joseph—Ted Kennedy cuts an iconic if somewhat tragic figure in the story of twentieth-century American politics. After attending elite preparatory schools, Kennedy was admitted to Harvard University. Expelled during his first term for cheating on an exam, he was eventually readmitted to Harvard and finally graduated in 1956.

Kennedy's political career began in 1962 when he was elected to fill the Senate seat formerly occupied by newly elected president John Kennedy. As a United States senator, Ted Kennedy's achievements are at least as impressive in number and scope as those of his older brothers. Kennedy's influential support played an important role in the Immigration and Nationality Act of 1965, which abolished national origin quotas. Closer to his ethnic heritage, Kennedy argued passionately for the creation of a united Ireland in 1971, claiming that nothing less than complete removal of all British troops in Northern Island could form the basis for national unity. He has consistently and very publicly supported a variety of progressive agendas, ranging from abortion rights and gun control to alternative energy programs and same-sex marriage rights. He is considered a master of persuasive backroom dealing by colleagues on both sides of the aisle. And with an unabated forty-five-year tenure in the U.S. Senate, Ted Kennedy is currently the body's longest serving member next to Senator Robert Byrd of West Virginia.

Two major events in Kennedy's life are worth noting insofar as they helped feed negative public perceptions about him leading up to his Liberty Baptist College address. The first event occurred in 1969 on Chappaquiddick Island near Martha's Vineyard.

Kennedy attended a party honoring several female aides who had worked on Robert Kennedy's presidential campaign run. As the party was winding down, Kennedy offered to give one of the honorees, Mary Jo Kopechne, a lift back to her hotel. While en route, the car Kennedy was driving careened out of control on Dike Bridge and tumbled into Poucha Pond below. Tragically, Kopechne drowned. Kennedy did not report the incident to the police until some twelve hours later, and only after he had consulted with his lawyers and family.

With suspicions mounting about his role in the Chappaquiddick affair, Kennedy delivered a televised address to the people of Massachusetts in which he cast himself as a victim of tragic circumstances that were beyond his control.

The car overturned in a deep pond and immediately filled with water. . . . But somehow I struggled for the surface alive. I made immediate and repeated efforts to save Mary Jo by diving into the strong and murky current but succeeded only in increasing my state of utter exhaustion and alarm.

Ultimately, Kopechne's death was ruled an accidental drowning, and Kennedy pled guilty to leaving the scene of an accident. The Chappaquiddick speech is credited with saving Kennedy's senatorial career. But if opponents' charges of "ruthless opportunism" could be dismissed to some extent as so much partisan dirt-mongering, the episode still left a lingering sour taste in the mouths of many Americans for years to come.

Another event that negatively affected Kennedy's public persona was a failed attempt at capturing the Democratic Party presidential nomination in 1980. Partly this was an almost inevitable result of trying to live up to the towering political legacy of brothers John and Robert. The problem extended to Ted Kennedy's public speaking style, characterized even by his friends as "hopelessly inarticulate," "garbled," and "undisciplined." His public speaking problems coupled with Democratic incumbent Jimmy Carter's resurgence during the Iran hostage crisis effectively undercut Kennedy's chances at winning his party's nomination. The extent to which these events affected Kennedy's persona is evidenced, as we will see and hear, in Kennedy's Liberty speech.

Notwithstanding his ineffective campaign rhetoric, Ted Kennedy is a capable public speaker. His emotional eulogy at the funeral of Robert F. Kennedy ranks as one of the most eloquent pieces of ceremonial rhetoric produced in the twentieth century. His remarkable address at the 1980 Democratic National Convention in which he laid out the ideological core of the Democratic Party in articulate, sublime tones is considered by some to be his finest oratorical hour. The speech offered in this chapter pitted Kennedy's iconic persona, intellectual acuity, and personal charm that had earned him many admirers on both sides of the political aisle against a spirited evangelical audience, providing a case study in how the content of a public speech can graft together the ostensibly varied interests of church and state in a way that offers hope for them to participate in a healthy rhetorical relationship in American-style democracy.

Theory of Content

At a general level, the content of a speech refers to that body of ideas and arguments transmitted by a speaker to produce rational and emotional effects on an audience.

It was Aristotle in his treatise *On Rhetoric* who originally formulated the basic ideas behind the art of public speaking, arguing that content works along three modes of persuasion. Effective speech content puts the speaker in a favorable light (*ethos*), provokes the right emotions (*pathos*), and carries the force of reason (*logos*). Each content mode is subject to artful variation, according to the needs, expectations, and demands of a given audience.

Ethos refers to a speaker's credibility as perceived by the audience. Aristotle noted that ethos takes several forms, including moral virtue or character, practical wisdom, and goodwill. The idea is that audiences are more likely to be influenced by a good person possessed of common sense who has their better interests at heart than they would by an apparently self-interested person of somewhat questionable moral character.

Other forms of ethos abound. Among these must be counted trustworthiness, competence, and charisma. One form not cited by Aristotle and often and overly cited by commentators of political persuasion is "likeability." I do not have the space to articulate properly the disdain I have for this idea, though it is probably true that likeable characters are easier to listen to than unlikeable characters. But compared to the lofty ideals of Aristotle and those who followed him, this form seems comparatively trite and needlessly reductive.

As we learned in the preceding chapter, the success of Ronald Reagan's *Challenger* address depended on the construction of two kinds of ethos. His presidential ethos gave him authority to make definitive statements about the future of our space program and the way it would continue to operate as the product of an open and honest democracy. His ethos as "national eulogist" gave Reagan license to speak in reverent tones about the astronauts and convey heartfelt sympathy to the bereaved families and confused schoolchildren. Clearly, "likeable" in this context just doesn't quite capture it.

Finally, it is important to distinguish between those qualities that a speaker may or may not *actually* possess and those that an audience *perceives* the speaker to possess. Ethos concerns only the latter. Ethos is cultivated specifically through what a speaker does (and does not) actually say to foster the appearance of these qualities. Most fundamentally, ethos is an effective mode of persuasion simply because we are more likely to be influenced by a speech if we are favorably disposed to the speaker. Ethos is a kind of bridge that encourages us to be receptive to a message on the basis of what we believe and how we feel about the speaker.

Pathos refers to the use of content to induce certain emotions in an audience. Our emotions influence our judgment, leading us to interpret and act upon ideas differently than we otherwise might. We have learned this from experiences closer to home, where ostensibly innocuous statements like "How was your day?" can serve as the catalyst for epic dramas, depending on our own and our partner's emotional states of mind. Good speakers exploit the emotional dimension of an audience to create a favorable emotional frame in which their ideas and arguments can be more readily accepted. Emotions, effectively engaged and managed, can influence our reception of a message.

Aristotle's treatment of emotions is astounding in scope. In *On Rhetoric*, one finds not merely a litany of emotions identified and defined but also rigorous formulations on how best to induce them. Anger, for example, is "desire, accompanied with pain, for conspicuous revenge for a conspicuous slight that was directed against oneself or those near to one, when such a slight is undeserved." The state of mind of a person who gets angry, the targets of that anger, and the various reasons for and motives underlying that anger must all be considered. Other emotions that may be of use to the speaker include mildness (the antithesis of anger), love and hatred, fear and confidence, shame and indifference, and pity and indignation.

Aristotle's treatment of pathos seems somewhat counterintuitive in that it uses rational methods to induce an emotional state. Most speakers are intuitively familiar with how emotions work and do not have to consider all the detail Aristotle's formulations require. Moreover, Aristotle does not consider the role that individual words and phrases can have on our emotions. Words such as "liberal" or "vast right-wing conspiracy" have the power to summon fervent emotions merely by their incantation. So while we can take Aristotle's cues regarding the role of pathos in persuasion, we must be sensitive to the varying ways a speaker may attempt to induce certain emotions in an audience.

The rational force, or *logos*, of content refers to the mix of main and supporting propositions that together bolster arguments calculated to win the reasonable assent of the audience. When addressing a disagreeable or even hostile audience, a speaker will often begin with certain ideas or propositions that are held in common agreement by all sides and use them as a point of departure to introduce more controversial ideas. The idea is to establish some common rational ground before moving to ground that is more readily contestable. A pro-life speaker addressing pro-choice advocates might begin by first stating and developing the idea that "Life is precious." This would seem to be a safe point of departure since it is unlikely that most people would argue its opposite, that "Life is not precious."

As content moves forward to more controversial ideas in a speech, propositions will require rational support. This support may be offered in the form of compelling reasons and authoritative evidence. The evidence itself may take the form of real or hypothetical examples, statistics, historical anecdotes, research reports, stories, analogies, and so forth.

When a proposition is given rational support, the entire unit becomes an "argument." "Smoking should be banned in all public restaurants" is a proposition but not yet an argument. As a proposition, its logical status may be a declaration of conviction, a self-evident truth, or even a command. Sometimes it is in the interest of a speaker merely to assert propositions without offering further support, especially if the proposition is not likely to engender serious debate. Politicians hot on the campaign trail are masters at using such propositions. "I believe that every American should be given the opportunity of a good education" is a dandy-sounding statement but hardly offers any ground for rational discussion. When is the last time you heard anyone argue seriously that "Every American should not be given the opportunity of a good education"?

When a debatable proposition is supported by at least one other proposition we have an argument. "Smoking should be banned in all public restaurants because it is deleterious to our health" is an argument. Of course, many arguments are not quite so simple. Here is a slightly more complex version of the argument: "Smoking should be banned in all public restaurants because, as the surgeon general duly warns us, it is bad for your health." The structure of this argument can be laid out as follows:

P1: According to the surgeon general, smoking is bad for your health.

P2: The surgeon general's opinion on matters of health is reliable.

C: Smoking should be banned in all public restaurants.

Here, we have three propositions. C is the main claim or conclusion of the argument. P1 is the primary premise supporting the conclusion, and P2 is the implied premise or "warrant" that authorizes the rational connection between P1 and the conclusion.

Changing the order of propositions does not usually affect the way the argument itself should be rationally considered. A speaker might say, "As the surgeon general duly warns, smoking should be banned in all public restaurants since it is deleterious to your health." The syntax of the argument has changed but its rational structure remains the same.

For purposes of clarity, it is often helpful to distinguish between main and supporting propositions with argument "cues." Words and phrases such as "therefore," "as a result," and "consequently" are useful ways to signal the main proposition, or conclusion, of an argument. For instance, "I don't like you and therefore can't marry you" is a simple argument whose conclusion about marriage is supported by the proposition about liking. Similarly, words and phrases like "because," "since," "on the grounds that," "on the evidence of," and "for the reason that" signal supporting propositions in an argument. But be on your guard. Speakers do not always use such words when introducing a proposition. Sometimes such words are used but not as cues to an argument.

Finally, it is important to consider how those arguments are grounded—from what appeals they issue. "Smoking should be banned from all public restaurants because it is bad for your health" and "Smoking should be banned from all public restaurants because it is against God's will" are both simple arguments but are grounded in different sources of appeal. The first appeals from a health standpoint, the second from religious conviction.

There are numerous sources of appeal, many of which can be used to defend or attack the same proposition. Common sources include general social categories such as economics, health, the law, and religion and commonly held values such as justice, mercy, patriotism, and inclusiveness. Less common but no less important are the appeals engendered from various philosophies, such as rugged individualism, utilitarianism, and pragmatism.

Rugged individualism, an all-American appeal, runs something like "I will do whatever I want, whenever I want, and however I want—period. I am a free-born American citizen and I am free! I'll smoke wherever I want to—period." Society would probably break down quite quickly if the force of this appeal were left unchecked. Fortunately, rugged individualism can be balanced by utilitarianism. A utilitarian appeal is based on the idea that we should only do those things that result in the greatest amount of good for the greatest number of people. Finally, pragmatism, a quintessential American philosophy, runs, "Only do things that will work." If a smoking ban is likely to meet with a great deal of protest—people still smoke in restaurants in defiance of the policy or people no longer eat out—then the policy probably won't work. With pragmatism, only policies that work or are likely to carry the day.

The Liberal Lion and the Moral Majority

The road that brought Ted Kennedy to Liberty Baptist College began, not altogether surprisingly, with a clerical error. Kennedy received a membership card from the Moral Majority, a politically minded conservative religious organization, thanking him for the financial support which, in fact, Kennedy had never given. Amused, Kennedy phoned Jerry Falwell, the group's founder and president, to thank him personally for the complimentary membership card. In the ensuing and apparently good-natured conversation between the two, Falwell invited Kennedy to address his university's faculty and student body on the subject of the relationship between politics and religion in America. To the surprise of many, Kennedy accepted. The event became something of a media flashpoint, as the liberal lion's agreement to venture out into a rival den of evangelicals was certainly news.

The Moral Majority was founded in 1979 on an ideology that trumpeted the inherent value of the family, patriarchically situated, as the cornerstone of a vibrant national order. It was pro-Israel, pro-life, anti-gun control, and against secular education. The organization is credited as a key factor in the successful 1980 presidential election campaign of Ronald Reagan by registering millions of first-time voters and lobbying numerous political officials to that end. By the time of Kennedy's address, Falwell and the Moral Majority presided over a substantial level of political and cultural influence from a deeply conservative religious base unequaled perhaps since before the days of the 1925 Scopes trial.

Liberty Baptist College was founded by Jerry Falwell in Lynchburg, Virginia, in 1971. Falwell, pastor of Thomas Road Baptist Church, began the Christian liberal arts school with the hope of eventually making it a "fundamentalist Harvard." Although the university's academic reputation has yet to rise to those lofty academic heights, it has been accredited by the Southern Association of Colleges and Schools since 1980. It was renamed Liberty University in 1985.

The student body at Liberty, since its inception, is, as a matter of religious faith tradition, largely fundamentalist Christian. Fundamentalist Christianity belongs to the more broadly based ideological movement known as "evangelicalism." In 1983, Liberty Baptist College only accepted students who formally acknowledged a "born-again" relationship with God. Dancing, drinking, and movies were forbidden. All 4,300 members of Liberty's student body took prescribed courses in religion in addition to their regular program of study and nearly one-quarter of these were studying for the ministry. By these measures, Kennedy was facing an audience ideologically hostile to him. As one student put it, "Kennedy represents everything that is wrong

with American society . . . the antithesis of good government, constitutional government, and Judeo-Christian
ethic." Falwell himself had been rumored to say that "some
of his people thought Kennedy was the 'devil incarnate.'"
And thus was the rhetorical table set for Kennedy's Liberty
Baptist College address.

"Tolerance and Truth"

Ted Kennedy faced a rhetorical situation with three pressing problems: an ideologically hostile audience, the perception of a disagreeably liberal message, and an ostensibly
devilish public persona. Thus, Kennedy's most immediate
rhetorical goal was to set an emotional tone that would
lighten the rhetorical load.

> *Thank you very much Professor Kombay for that
> generous introduction. And let me say that I never
> expected to hear such kind words from Dr. Falwell.
> So in return, I have an invitation of my own. On
> January 20, 1985, I hope Dr. Falwell will say a
> prayer at the inauguration of the next Democratic
> President of the United States. Now, Dr. Falwell,
> I'm not exactly sure how you feel about that. You
> might not appreciate the President, but the Democrats
> certainly would appreciate the prayer.*
>
> *Actually, a number of people in Washington were
> surprised that I was invited to speak here—and
> even more surprised when I accepted the invitation.
> They seem to think that it's easier for a camel to pass
> through the eye of the needle than for a Kennedy
> to come to the campus of Liberty Baptist College.*

> *In honor of our meeting, I have asked Dr. Falwell,*
> *as your Chancellor, to permit all the students an*
> *extra hour next Saturday night before curfew. And*
> *in return, I have promised to watch the "Old Time*
> *Gospel Hour" next Sunday morning.*
>
> *I realize that my visit may be a little controversial.*
> *But as many of you have heard, Dr. Falwell recently*
> *sent me a membership in the Moral Majority—and I*
> *didn't even apply for it. And I wonder if that means*
> *that I'm a member in good standing. . . .*
>
> *This is, of course, a nonpolitical speech, which is*
> *probably best under the circumstances. Since I am*
> *not a candidate for president, it would certainly be*
> *inappropriate to ask for your support in this election*
> *and probably inaccurate to thank you for it in the last*
> *one.*

Kennedy's first content tactic is pathos. With a series of strategically targeted, lighthearted jokes, Kennedy puts his very serious-minded audience into a less guarded state of mind. The first joke comes at the expense of the Democratic Party, the second at the expense of his family (or perhaps the mystique associated with the family name), and the final two at the expense of himself. Thus, in a few brief moments of content, Kennedy has "taken out" the rhetorical force associated with three of the most vilified objects of his audience's disdain.

By using self-effacing humor, Kennedy constructs a positive ethos in order to establish a measure of goodwill. The content of the joke about prayer is audience empowering, even in the guise of humor, in that Kennedy is soliciting it from them on his party's behalf. It is appropriate that among the various and variously divisive religious activities that separate church from state, prayer is not among them. Prayer is a universally acceptable form of behavior and one in which all sides can find some common ground. The U.S. Senate is no exception.

Also to be noted is Kennedy's successful baiting of Falwell himself. Kennedy's question about his own standing in the Moral Majority—a question posed only indirectly— tempts Falwell into the response, "Somewhat," that makes him a participant in Kennedy's construction of goodwill and provides further cause for his audience to fall in line with their leader's act of beneficence. As is sometimes noted, real power is the power to exercise a judgment of mercy when condemnation is otherwise forthcoming. Thus, Kennedy secures not merely goodwill, but a particularly powerful kind of goodwill that comes only when an audience believes they are empowered on their own terms. By these content tactics, Kennedy upholds the appearance of the presiding situational powers that be.

Finally, by appearing to compromise some of his own power—taking shots at his party, family, and himself— Kennedy is establishing important logical groundwork for the substance of his message to follow. Namely, both powers will have to come to some compromise if they have any chance of dining together peacefully at democracy's table. And that compromise will necessarily involve relinquishing some claims to power. As Kennedy's content models, such compromise can and should be done in a spirit of good humor. By these means has the lion gentled the lambs, and, to all present appearances, the gates of heaven are, if not prevailing, at least standing firm.

I have come here to discuss my beliefs about faith and country, tolerance and truth in America. I

know we begin with certain disagreements; I strongly
suspect that at the end of the evening some of our
disagreements will remain. But I also hope that
tonight and in the months and years ahead, we will
always respect the right of others to differ, that we will
never lose sight of our own fallibility, that we will
view ourselves with a sense of perspective and a sense
of humor. After all, in the New Testament, even the
Disciples had to be taught to look first to the beam
in their own eyes, and only then to the mote in their
neighbor's eyes.

Kennedy has now twice alluded to scripture to make a point. The first instance is a passing remark about the improbability of his attendance at Liberty, which, given the outcome, provides some cause for reconsidering the odds actually facing a camel's foray into a needle's eye. The second reference to the Bible betrays a more serious bait-and-switch design. To this point, Kennedy had lured the audience into a sense of comfort by appealing to their sense of religious security. Without warning, he then thumps that security on its righteous head with the biblical admonition not to judge. The effect must have produced something of a gestalt switch. Kennedy, that most liberal of lions, has styled himself a conservative shepherd, gently chiding his audience to remain faithful to their spiritual roots by giving the situation an open and honest hearing.

With ethos and pathos initially established, Kennedy moves the audience onto more rational footing.

I am an American and a Catholic; I love my country
and treasure my faith. But I do not assume that

*my conception of patriotism or policy is invariably
correct, or that my convictions about religion should
command any greater respect than any other faith in
this pluralistic society. I believe there surely is such
a thing as truth, but who among us can claim a
monopoly on it?*

Someone has said that "there are two kinds of people in the
world: those who think in binary and those who don't." It
is perhaps our cognitive nature to gravitate toward comfortable dichotomies, either-or thinking that reduces our
worlds into manageable, albeit simplistic, categories of
thought. Evangelicals, however, are particularly faithful adherents to dichotomous thinking of a starkly moral
kind. Categories of good versus evil, light versus darkness,
saint versus sinner, and saved versus lost become compelling and primary filters through which reality takes on
its particular evangelical color, one that tends to discourage more open and nuanced views of reality—particularly
important when that reality happens to be relatively open
and nuanced.

Kennedy's self-identifications as "American" and
"Catholic" function as labels that encourage the audience
to focus on two and only two categories of the speaker's
identity and away from extraneous or otherwise unhelp-
ful ones. But there is more going on in terms of logos.
Conjoining the terms "Catholic" and "American" with the
conjunction "and" is a logical tactic designed to begin the
process of carving out a public rhetorical space in which
the relationship between politics and religion can be mutually considered. In running together "love my country"
and "treasure my faith," Kennedy undermines the false
either-or dichotomy to which many in his audience would

initially be tempted: namely, you are either Protestant and American—or not. Consequently, Kennedy's content unifies both Protestant and Catholic under those who "treasure their faith" and alongside a banner of patriotism. The very reasonable conclusion is that Protestants and Catholics are both fully American. Kennedy's content tactic uses logos both to encourage and to discourage the human temptation to think in simple dichotomous categories in ways favorable to his primary message of tolerance. But there is more rational work to be done in the effort to mitigate religious intolerance.

> *There are those who do, and their own words testify*
> *to their intolerance. For example, because the Moral*
> *Majority has worked with members of different*
> *denominations, one fundamentalist group has*
> *denounced Dr. Falwell for hastening the ecumenical*
> *church and for "yoking together with Roman*
> *Catholics, Mormons, and others." I am relieved that*
> *Dr. Falwell does not regard that as a sin, and on*
> *this issue, he himself has become the target of narrow*
> *prejudice. When people agree on public policy, they*
> *ought to be able to work together, even while they*
> *worship in diverse ways. For truly we are all yoked*
> *together as Americans, and the yoke is the happy one*
> *of individual freedom and mutual respect.*

Here, logos works simply by combining a proposition about intolerance with a simple example supporting the proposition. We now have an argument that runs, "Religion has been guilty of intolerance on the grounds that some of the Moral Majority have been charged with unchristian ecumenicalism." The example is also emotionally compelling in that it is drawn from the same religious tradition, evangelicalism, as his audience and thereby rationally and emotionally compels the audience to come to terms with the question of who the real enemy is. And that enemy cannot be reduced to simplistic categories of politics or religion because it recognizes no political or religious barriers. The real enemy is intolerance and it can strike anywhere, anytime, against anyone.

There is an additional pathos ploy at work here whose effect is best felt in real-time listening. The first sentence in the segment above is cleverly crafted to stimulate Kennedy's evangelical audience to moral judgment. The phrase "those who do" offers a tantalizingly vague and thus unsatisfying target for that judgment. Moral judgment requires a definitive target for the concrete imputation of guilt. With his audience's moral senses now alerted, Kennedy identifies the Moral Majority itself as the apparent culprit. (If you listen to or read this segment from its beginning and pause at the term "Moral Majority," that would be the impression.) Kennedy is teasing his audience with the unpleasant taste of collective guilt before washing away the taste by transferring it onto another group.

Of course, a single example does not an entire generalization prove. The term "hasty generalization" refers to a logical fallacy in which an entire group is characterized on the basis of a limited number of its members. To bolster the argument about intolerance, more examples will be needed and more examples Kennedy provides.

The founders of our nation had long and bitter experience with the state, as both the agent and the adversary of particular religious views. In colonial Maryland, Catholics paid a double land tax, and

*in Pennsylvania they had to list their names on
a public roll—an ominous precursor of the first
Nazi laws against the Jews. And Jews in turn
faced discrimination in all of the thirteen original
colonies. Massachusetts exiled Roger Williams and
his congregation for contending that civil government
had no right to enforce the Ten Commandments.
Virginia harassed Baptist teachers and also established
a religious test for public service, writing into the law
that no "popish followers" could hold any office.*

Kennedy assumes the burden of proof on the charge that
his audience's evangelical faith has been specially singled
out for institutionalized, secular oppression. The content
tactic of varied and abundant examples, presented in rapid-
fire succession, is designed to overwhelm that charge. Having established the proposition that intolerance is not the
special province of religion or government, Kennedy's next
argument centers on what happens when a certain religious
faith tradition is singled out for special consideration.

*The separation of church and state can sometimes be
frustrating for women and men of religious faith.
They may be tempted to misuse government in order
to impose a value which they cannot persuade others
to accept. But once we succumb to that temptation,
we step onto a slippery slope where everyone's freedom
is at risk. Those who favor censorship should recall
that one of the first books ever burned was the
first English translation of the Bible. As President
Eisenhower warned in 1953, "Don't join the book
burners. . . . the right to say ideas, the right to record
them, and the right to have them accessible to others*

is unquestioned—or this isn't America." And if that right is denied, at some future day the torch can be turned against any other book or any other belief. Let us never forget: Today's Moral Majority could become tomorrow's persecuted minority.

The argument here, again supported by way of examples, is that the political favoring of a single religious tradition puts all religious traditions at the mercy of their political maker(s). Pathos, too, is employed in the appeal to fear. If religious oppression can happen to any faith, it can happen to the evangelical faith. Kennedy continues to press the appeal.

The danger is as great now as when the founders of the nation first saw it. In 1789, their fear was of factional strife among dozens of denominations. Today there are hundreds—and perhaps even thousands—of faiths and millions of Americans who are outside any fold. Pluralism obviously does not and cannot mean that all of them are right; but it does mean that there are areas where government cannot and should not decide what it is wrong to believe, to think, to read, and to do. As Professor Larry Tribe, one of the nation's leading constitutional scholars has written, "Law in a nontheocratic state cannot measure religious truth, nor can the state impose it."
The real transgression occurs when religion wants government to tell citizens how to live uniquely personal parts of their lives.

The appeal to fear takes on an added dimension, rationally supported by "one of the nation's leading constitutional scholars." Not only are we to fear a government that would decide which religion is correct or sponsor one particular religion over and against all others, but we should equally fear a religious faith tradition that would influence its government to dictate certain religious values to its citizens.

At no other time does Kennedy tread on more dangerous rhetorical ground. The term "uniquely personal parts of their lives" signals a potentially divisive distinction between the public and the private. Interestingly enough, this is one dichotomy that evangelicals are hard-pressed to accept, not because their faith is less than personal but because their faith is understood to be both private and public. This is a natural extension of the evangelical conviction to share one's religious faith with a "lost and dying world." The political parallel to this religious conviction is what gave evangelicals the impetus to vote for a politician in Ronald Regan who would openly advocate the public, political expression of religious faith.

To ward off the danger, Kennedy next suggests that some questions of a definitively public nature are indeed in play for religious consideration, specifically those questions that would require a moral basis for response.

> But there are other questions which are inherently
> public in nature, which we must decide together as a
> nation, and where religion and religious values can
> and should speak to our common conscience. The issue
> of nuclear war is a compelling example. It is a moral
> issue; it will be decided by government, not by each
> individual; and to give any effect to the moral values
> of their creed, people of faith must speak directly about
> public policy. The Catholic bishops and the Reverend
> Billy Graham have every right to stand for the nuclear

*freeze, and Dr. Falwell has every right to stand
against it.*

Kennedy here simply begs the most important question his audience would have: by what principle(s) should we distinguish between those public questions which religious faith may and may not properly address? The appeal to "common conscience" is a pleasant-sounding abstraction but likely carries no rational force with an audience whose values are by right of scripture. Graham and Falwell may well disagree on a nuclear freeze but how does that disagreement get his audience any closer to determining which questions are and are not in play for religious faith?

Kennedy has probably reached the limits of what rational argument can accomplish with this particular audience. And while the final section in which Kennedy offers four rational principles for cultivating a healthy relationship between religion and politics does offer rational grounds, the explanation of how these principles might actually serve uniquely evangelical interests is far from clear.

The principles, however, do carry persuasive force grounded in an ethos of goodwill. In calling for parties of different religious and political convictions to respect "the integrity of religion," "public debate," our "independent judgments of conscience," and the "motives of those who . . . disagree," Kennedy has succeeded in presenting himself in this rhetorical situation as something decidedly less than the "devil incarnate." And although the temptation of Jesus finds the devil to be a willing and capable user of biblical scripture, Kennedy's closing quotation of Paul the Apostle's admonition to "live peaceably with all men" offers a compelling ethos for this particular lion's willingness to lie down with the lambs.

4

Structure

Douglas MacArthur's Thayer Award Acceptance Address

As ANY HALF-BAKED new recruit quickly learns, disciplined structure is the lifeblood of any successfully functioning military outfit from unit to platoon to company to battalion to brigade to division to corps—all of the building blocks must be in lockstep order for the army to work. Likewise, great oration, while displaying more variety and offering considerably more freedom in arrangement, often succeeds or fails, as with any military endeavor, according to how well its various parts fit together into a unified whole.

In 1962, eighty-two-year-old Douglas MacArthur accepted the Sylvanus Thayer Award at the United States Military Academy at West Point, New York. One of the greatest military ceremonial speeches in history, it demonstrates a mastery of rhetorical structure. While this distinction is due in part to its sheer eloquence of diction, it owes perhaps as much to the general's subtle but strategically structured progression of ideas and images that guided his audience of cadets and officers from one rhetorical vision to the next. To the extent that the speech was a "symphony of war-weary images and battle-tested tonalities," it was so only insofar as the arrangement of its three main movements kept those images and tonalities in lockstep order, building to a final crescendo that MacArthur's audience would not soon forget.

Douglas MacArthur

Douglas MacArthur (January 26, 1880–April 5, 1964) was born in Little Rock, Arkansas, to Arthur and Mary MacArthur. His father, a lieutenant general in the army, was a Civil War hero and recipient of the Congressional Medal of Honor. Douglas MacArthur entered the United States Military Academy in 1899 and graduated first in his class in 1903. Upon graduation, he entered the U.S. Army as a commissioned second lieutenant in the U.S. Army Corps of Engineers.

MacArthur's military career was prolific and included distinguished service in both world wars. In 1916, he became the first public relations officer in the U.S. Army. It was here that MacArthur gained a reputation for issuing military communiqués that were notable for their unseemly "purple" flourishes. The charge of inappropriate ornateness in his public written and spoken comments would dog MacArthur for years to come. Following the surrender of Japan in 1945, MacArthur oversaw the inaugural reconstruction efforts aimed at democratization, a nation-building effort credited with instituting a democratic government and capitalist economy.

His final military campaign during the Korean War saw MacArthur run afoul of President Harry Truman over a proposed strategic bombing of targets within China. Truman relieved MacArthur of his duties, and MacArthur retired. He returned home a hero in the eyes of many Americans. A highly decorated military officer, MacArthur was awarded the Congressional Medal of Honor, Distinguished Service Crosses from both the army and navy, a Purple Heart, and six Silver Stars among a bevy of other medals and badges.

In March of 1964, MacArthur was admitted to Walter Reed General Hospital complaining of "damned itching." Diagnosed with cirrhosis of the liver, the eighty-four-year-old MacArthur died three weeks later.

According to those who worked with him, MacArthur was a man given to appearances, having a theatrical sense about himself and his role in the world. Often intentionally intimidating, he could be stubborn to the point of obstinacy, critical to the point of humiliation, and seemingly incapable of admitting even small mistakes. His capacity for self-promotion earned him many critics, a point that Dwight Eisenhower noted with concern, saying that the most important lesson learned under MacArthur was "how to act." The general, it seems, was nothing if not an actor.

Given his self-possession, it is not surprising MacArthur's speeches were criticized for rhetorical excess—spates of flowery oratory calculated to draw attention to itself well beyond what the subject matter or occasion warranted. It was the tendency toward self-congratulatory oratory that his critics most keenly detested. When constrained, however, MacArthur's rhetoric could be entirely convincing, as was the case with his speech to the Joint Chiefs of Staff that resulted in the OK for attack at Inch'on, one of the most effective campaigns of the Korean War. MacArthur's farewell address to Congress, in which he spoke the immortal words "old soldiers never die; they just fade away," was one the finest military speeches delivered in the twentieth century and is another example of the restrained eloquence to which MacArthur's oratory could rise.

MacArthur's oratory reflected the best and worst of his nature. At its best, his style was stately, elevating his subject matter to heroic heights of eloquence that few of his peers could match. At its worst, his rhetoric could be self-indulgent and gratuitous to the point of absurdity. Fortunately, the speech under consideration here falls, with hardly an exception, in the former category. Moreover, although MacArthur did not abide the criticism of others particularly well, he was with respect to his major addresses his own worst critic. As public speaker, MacArthur was particularly careful to remember certain passages in his speeches that elicited favorable responses from an audience. Over time, MacArthur polished and committed to memory a number of stock phrases, which could be called up on a moment's notice and inserted within the structure of a given speech. In his Thayer Award acceptance, we have a rhetorically mature MacArthur who is able to meet the requirements of the rhetorical situation in a way the younger MacArthur could only have envied.

Theory of Structure

It has been said that "matter without form is meaningless": raw materials must be shaped before they can have value. Star-crossed lovers have little shortage of material when considering the object of their affections, but it takes a skillful songwriter to arrange that material in the form of verses and choruses capable of communicating that affection meaningfully to the masses. Visionaries may think in the abstract of how individual liberty might be associated with a bunch of stars here and a dozen stripes there, but citizens will speak of their liberty with pointed patriotism only insofar as those stars and stripes appear on a rectangular field containing a smaller blue rectangle in the upper left quadrant bearing fifty white stars offset by thirteen horizontal alternating red and white stripes in the remainder of the field. Absent this particular structure of stars and stripes, Americans would have no official "seal" for our hard-earned liberty—the American flag.

And so it goes with the relationship between the content and structure of a speech. While the structure of national flags and pop songs do not in themselves provide a working model for public speeches—there is no speech equivalent for the heralded *aaba* structure in popular songs—the fact that the raw materials of a public speech must have a discernible structure in order to maximize its effectiveness does. In the beginning, darkness covers the face of a speech until it is given discernible form.

There are two basic ways to think of the structure of a speech: "macrostructure" and "microstructure." The macrostructure of a speech concerns the large-scale division of content into three general parts: introduction, body, and conclusion. The microstructure of a speech concerns the division of these three general parts into smaller units or subsections. Just how many subsections are involved for a given speech will vary considerably by factors such as subject, audience, occasion, and speaker preference, among other things.

Most introductions attempt to establish a measure of rapport with the audience. Identifying commonly held traits or circumstances is a typical tactic used to establish common ground. Another common tactic for achieving rapport is found in the use of an idea or person to which the audience stands in opposition. Here it is a common distrust, distaste, or dislike of someone or something that forms the basis for the speaker-audience bond. More positively, humor can be a particularly effective tactic. In revisiting our lessons from the previous chapter, we note some seven instances of the use of humor in Edward Kennedy's speech at Liberty Baptist College in the introduction alone!

In addition to rapport, the microstructure of a speech introduction typically includes a preview of the subject matter to be addressed in the body of the speech, the identification of the purpose of and/or goals for the speech, and the establishment of the speaker's identity and relationship to the subject matter. As we will see in Chapter 6, Barbara Jordan identified herself as an unlikely "inquisitor" in relation to the question of presidential impeachment during the House Judiciary proceedings of May 1972.

Material in the body of a speech is generally arranged according to some principle of progression. Common progression principles include *chronological, topical,* and *problem-solution.* Material is arranged chronologically when it is conveyed as a series of events occurring in time such as a story or narrative. Topical arrangement takes a point of discussion such as the function of the U.S. Armed Forces and divides it up into smaller manageable units: Army, Navy, Air Force, and Marines. Problem-solution format allows for a discussion of problems and their significance, a detailed explication of the plausible solutions, a consideration of alternative solutions, and an assessment of the new problems that will accrue if a given solution is taken.

Microstructural elements in the conclusion of a speech generally include an indication that the speech is about to close ("In conclusion"), a reinforcement of the main purpose of the speech, and a sense of closure.

One final structural point requires mentioning. It is an unhappy fact that audiences weary of words all too quickly. Typically, they remember less than 50 percent of the content in a speech—sometimes much less than that. The mind wanders—the postmodern mind all too easily. As a partial remedy to this problem, a "structural motif" may be employed. A structural motif is a recurring phrase or word unit that captures the central theme of a speech. Its purpose is to refocus the mind at key intervals during the speech. MacArthur will make ample use of this structural tactic through his thirty-five-minute address.

To summarize, the content of a speech is organized on macrostructural and microstructrural levels. The macrostructure of most speeches includes a more or less generic introduction, body, and conclusion. Within these parts, microstructural elements come into play. In the introduction, speakers may establish rapport, preview the subject matter, and establish the speaker's identity and relationship to the subject matter. Content in the body of the speech progresses along one or more patterns of arrangement, including chronological, topical, and problem-solution. A conclusion typically signals the end of the speech, summarizes the main material to be remembered, and provides the audience with a sense of closure. Following the next section, we will see how the structure of MacArthur's speech works hand in glove with its content to move the audience.

Returning to West Point

Created in 1958 and named after a brigadier general, the Thayer Award is given each year at the United States Military Academy at West Point to "an outstanding citizen of the United States whose service and accomplishments in the national interest exemplify personal devotion to the ideals expressed in the West Point motto, 'Duty, Honor, Country.'" MacArthur was the fifth person to receive the award. Previous recipients were Dr. Ernest O. Lawrence (1958), John Foster Dulles (1959), and Henry Cabot Lodge (1960). Dwight D. Eisenhower had received the award the previous year. Future recipients of the award would include President Ronald Reagan and Congressperson Barbara Jordan.

MacArthur arrived in the morning dressed in a dark business suit and wearing a homburg hat. As part of the festivities, MacArthur inspected the Corps of Cadets on the old parade ground standing rigid in the passenger cabin of a military jeep as the cadets marched by in gleaming, full-saber salute. Following a formal luncheon at Washington Hall, Lieutenant General Leslie Groves, president of the Association of Graduates, formally presented General Douglas MacArthur with the fifth annual Sylvanus Thayer Award for his outstanding and exemplary service to the nation.

There is some controversy associated with the delivery of the speech. In his autobiography, MacArthur declares he had no prepared address for the occasion. In view of this,

MacArthur's extemporaneous delivery was merely a summation of the U.S. Army's code and a lifetime's worth of living it. At least one biographer notes the presence of passages in the address that appeared in previous speeches by MacArthur, a not altogether unusual pattern for seasoned speakers who care about the craft and especially about the legacy their rhetoric leaves. Lou Sullivan, an associate of MacArthur's, recalls him "pacing like a brooding hawk through his ten-room apartment, puffing a corncob [pipe] while he rehearsed."

However the speech may have been prepared, commentators are unanimous in their praise of it. Its effect was called "mesmerizing" on the immediate audience, many of whom began listening with respectful silence and ended up openly weeping as the speech drew to a close. As military ceremonial speeches go, MacArthur's Thayer Award acceptance is one of the finest rhetorical achievements in American history.

Duty, Honor, Country

The macrostructure of MacArthur's address follows a general pattern of introduction, body, and conclusion. In the introduction, MacArthur identifies key authority figures in the audience. Next, he grabs attention and establishes rapport through a brief, humorous anecdote that also draws an important line between insiders and outsiders. Finally, by locating the significance of the award in the meaning of its "code," MacArthur previews the content of the body of his speech while also establishing the code's relationship to him as speaker. In this way, MacArthur fulfills the structural requirements often found in the introduction to a ceremonial speech.

The body of this speech is divided into four ideas arranged topically. The first two microsections concern the significance of the award as embodied in the code itself. The second microsection deals with the code's application to the officer and the soldier. There is some back and forth maneuvering between the main points, and clearly MacArthur returns to earlier ideas in the body for purposes of reinforcement and clarification.

Finally, MacArthur's conclusion sums up his thoughts on his military career and offers a final call to those who are about to embark upon theirs.

The content of the speech is illustrated by this outline:

I. Introduction

    1. Salutation
    2. Attention/Rapport
    3. Preview/Credibility

II. Body

    1. Meaning of the Code
    2. Value of the Code
    3. Honor of the Soldier
    4. Duty of the Soldier

III. Conclusion

    1. Stir of Echoes

Introduction

General Westmoreland, General Grove, distinguished guests, and gentlemen of the Corps!

MacArthur's introduction invokes an opening salut typical of ceremonial speeches marking formal ⌐⌐⌐a- sions. The audience is divided into sections, with the most important members identified in order by title and name. The remaining members of the audience are identified by group, using formal but positive group labels. Such open- ing gestures are an important way to mark the formality of the occasion and should as a rule be used whenever possible. It gives cause for each member of the audience to feel personally addressed by the speaker and gives each member a due sense of place in relation to other audience members. In this way MacArthur marks his rhetorical ter- ritory, what might be called the microstructural element of "territory marking."

> *As I was leaving the hotel this morning, a doorman asked me, "Where are you bound for, General?" And when I replied, "West Point," he remarked, "Beautiful place. Have you ever been there before?"*

MacArthur next establishes rapport of a fraternal kind, a bond among privileged insiders of a great and vener- able institution. The general's anecdote understates the privilege but captures the point. The audience's discern- ible laughter comes at the expense of the casual question of an outsider far removed from the reality of the fraternal bond. It is as though the only decent thing to do is to cast it off as a humorous aside. But an important line dividing insiders and outsiders has been drawn, and the old general has drawn it.

MacArthur has something else up his sleeve. Unknown to his audience at the time, MacArthur has in a rhetori- cal sense set them up. The opening quip will be the only

lighthearted moment the general will permit himself and
his audience over the entire terrain of the speech. From
this view, it is a momentarily buoyant moment in what
will become a sea of deep emotion. It is as though the
old general has gazed upon his charges and given them
a knowing wink of the eye before entering the bowels of
an address where heroic rhetorical battle will be waged.
From this view, the joke is not as much *for* them as it is
on them. The opening levity quickly gives way to a much
deeper level of engagement between MacArthur and his
audience.

> *No human being could fail to be deeply moved by*
> *such a tribute as this [Thayer Award]. Coming from*
> *a profession I have served so long, and a people I have*
> *loved so well, it fills me with an emotion I cannot*
> *express. But this award is not intended primarily to*
> *honor a personality, but to symbolize a great moral*
> *code—the code of conduct and chivalry of those*
> *who guard this beloved land of culture and ancient*
> *descent. That is the animation of this medallion.*
> *For all eyes and for all time, it is an expression of*
> *the ethics of the American soldier. That I should be*
> *integrated in this way with so noble an ideal arouses*
> *a sense of pride and yet of humility which will be*
> *with me always.*

In the final part of the introduction, MacArthur establishes his relationship to the subject at hand and previews
the content to follow. The award is deeply moving but not
primarily as a matter of personal honor. Rather, its honor is
contained in a code of chivalry antithetical to self-seeking

adulation, a point to which MacArthur had been sensi‍
and a lesson he wanted to make sure to impress upon the
cadets.

Too, this is the first of several times that MacArthur
will use an age-old ploy designed to disarm the listener
and curry favor with the audience. The phrase "filled
with an emotion I cannot express" is a variant of the
"unaccustomed as I am to speaking" figure of feigned
oratorical incompetence. Its use dates at least as far back
as the great Athenian oratory of the golden age in which
a speaker would typically state his inability to find words
that eventually would be found. Its use goes to humility
and goodwill, two important dimensions of credibility,
particularly where MacArthur is concerned. To those
acquainted with the younger MacArthur and who shared
Eisenhower's opinion that MacArthur had fashioned
himself as a leading actor in plays of his own making,
the ploy may seem disingenuous. MacArthur was never
known for lowering any bar, certainly not the bar of oratorical excellence.

The sweeping and self-referential terms "no human," "I
have loved so long," and "I have served so well" delivered
by a younger and more assured MacArthur would have
provided fodder for his critics as another sign of unbri-
dled self-possession. Here, however, they strike an utterly
convincing tone of deeply felt reverence. In listening to
this speech, you will have by now been struck by the pal-
pable frailty in MacArthur's voice. If you compare this
delivery with that of his farewell to Congress address you
will quickly get a sense of MacArthur's commanding—
even overbearing at times—verbal delivery. The toll that
MacArthur's advancing years took on his voice together

with his structured eloquence lend to the speech an utterly convincing integrity.

Body: Meaning of the Code

> *Duty, Honor, Country: Those three hallowed words reverently dictate what you ought to be, what you can be, what you will be. They are your rallying points: to build courage when courage seems to fail; to regain faith when there seems to be little cause for faith; to create hope when hope becomes forlorn. Unhappily, I possess neither that eloquence of diction, that poetry of imagination, nor that brilliance of metaphor to tell you all that they mean.*

Within the topical arrangement of the body, MacArthur begins by styling the great moral code in three words: "Duty, Honor, Country." He will repeat this code seven times over the course of the speech, in effect turning it into a structural motif. As mentioned previously, the motif is a structural strategy designed to capture the main thrust of the speech's overall theme by casting it in a short word unit. Content can be better recalled by merely stating a motif, but if MacArthur would have anything remembered he was going to make sure it was the call of the great moral code.

We may note something more about the motif. It is styled in *triplicate asyndeton*, a figure of expression in which three words with the same or close to the same number of syllables are set off by omitting a normally occurring conjunction, here the conjunction "and" before "country." Its deployment punctuates concision with ramrod-like clarity. It is an impassioned figure meant to signal the strength of the unit as a whole. Whereas "Duty, Honor, *and* Country" makes the latter term seem somewhat aloof from the former two, omitting the conjunction signals the strength of a tightly knit rhetorical team. The effect is ably demonstrated in other well-known configurations in military rhetoric from Julius Caesar's "Veni, vidi, vici" (I came, I saw, I conquered) to the U.S. Marine Corps's own rhetorical call to arms "The Few, the Proud, the Marines."

Indeed, MacArthur moves to invest the code with a transcendent moral significance that at first borders on and then crosses over into a kind of religious fervor. Reverence for the "three hallowed words" builds courage, regains faith, and even creates hope. This use closely parallels the well-known three-part New Testament phrase involving "faith, hope, and love" with the latter term removed in favor of "courage," which for obvious reasons is much better suited to the demands of the soldier's battle. If the suggestion of religious fervor of the code remains unconvincing, one need only to listen in the next section for MacArthur's lurid description of those who fail to understand the code as "unbelievers." MacArthur indeed moves beyond the merely moral implications of the code by wrapping morality with the power of religious conviction.

The sentence beginning "Unhappily, I possess neither" is MacArthur's second use of the oratorical incompetence ploy, stated quite eloquently using balanced parallelisms "eloquence of diction," "poetry of imagination," and "brilliance of metaphor." It is both emotionally resonant and self-defeating because of its eloquence. What else are we to make of a speaker who eloquently denies his own eloquence? Again, however, this ploy is used expressly for the purpose of currying goodwill with the audience in order to prepare the way for the rhetorical flourishes that follow.

*unbelievers will say they are but words, but
a slogan, but a flamboyant phrase. Every pedant,
every demagogue, every cynic, every hypocrite, every
troublemaker, and I am sorry to say, some others of
an entirely different character, will try to downgrade
them even to the extent of mockery and ridicule.*

Notions of "the good" are defined in part by what the good
stands against—what it is not. "Every hero requires a vil-
lain." In staking out enemy territory, MacArthur provides
a litany of villains against which the code and its heroes
must fight. Particularly effective here is the use of abstractions as opposed to specific names. Abstractions of evil
are rhetorically useful because they encourage the mind
to fill in the meaning with personally significant concrete
particulars. Moreover, these particular evils are universal
in human experience. In this way, MacArthur invests the
code with positive meaning and oppositional associations.
The stage is now set for the battle to come.

Body: Value of the Code

*But these are some of the things they [these words]
do. They build your basic character. They mold you
for your future roles as the custodians of the nation's
defense. They make you strong enough to know when
you are weak, and brave enough to face yourself
when you are afraid. They teach you to be proud and
unbending in honest failure, but humble and gentle
in success. . . . They give you a temper of the will, a
quality of the imagination, a vigor of the emotions, a*

freshness of the deep springs of life, a temperamental predominance of courage over timidity, of an appetite for adventure over love of ease. They create in your heart the sense of wonder, the unfailing hope of what next, and the joy and inspiration of life. They teach you in this way to be an officer and a gentleman.

Having set the stage, MacArthur prepares his officers for the kind of battle that must be fought. His is a territory of stark yet powerful moral contrasts. Here we find strength versus weakness, fortitude versus timidity, honest self-assessment versus hypocritical judgment. There is no middle ground. The officer's code can neither be compromised nor can it abide those who would seek its compromise. Armed with such knowledge, the gentlemen-officer is now qualified to lead. But lead whom? More than mere moral integrity is required as a pre-condition of leadership. One must also have a properly reverent understanding of the soldiers that the officer will lead. The soldier as an ideal is possessed of inherent value, and it is to that value that MacArthur next turns.

Body: Honor of the Soldier

And what sort of soldiers are those you are to lead? Are they reliable? Are they brave? Are they capable of victory? Their story is known to all of you. It is the story of the American man-at-arms. My estimate of him was formed on the battlefield many, many years ago, and has never changed. I regarded him then as I regard him now—as one of the world's noblest figures,

> *not only as one of the finest military characters, but
> also as one of the most stainless. . . . But when I think
> of his patience under adversity, of his courage under
> fire, and of his modesty in victory, I am filled with an
> emotion of admiration I cannot put into words. . . . I
> do not know the dignity of their birth, but I do know
> the glory of their death. They died unquestioning,
> uncomplaining, with faith in their hearts, and on
> their lips the hope that we would go on to victory.
> Always, for them: Duty, Honor, Country; always their
> blood and sweat and tears, as we sought the way and
> the light and the truth.*

The soldier is worthy of honor because of an inherent nobility. The soldier is honored as "one of the world's noblest figures" who displays reliability in "his patience under adversity" and bravery in his "courage under fire." MacArthur thus connects the first two terms in the code: the soldier is honored through the noble manner in which he carries out his duty.

MacArthur also trades on the storied role of honor in relation to death. Death is a particularly poignant aspect of the soldier's reality. MacArthur is both witness to and partaker of the soldier's honor, thereby becoming inextricably bound with the glory of the soldier. Not just any death will do, however. Honor is bestowed not merely because one dies for country but also because of the principles for which one dies—with heart full of faith and with hope on their lips. The soldier gains further honor by what his leaders say. MacArthur serves an example of how to honor the American soldier. He has witnessed the soldier carry out his solemn duty "on a hundred battlefields" with "enduring fortitude," "patriotic self-abnegation," and "invincible determination."

Body: Duty of the Soldier

Others will debate the controversial issues, national and international, which divide men's minds; but serene, calm, aloof, you stand as the nation's war-guardian, as its lifeguard from the raging tides of international conflict, as its gladiator in the arena of battle. For a century and a half you have defended, guarded, and protected its hallowed traditions of liberty and freedom, of right and justice. Let civilian voices argue the merits or demerits of our processes of government. . . . These great national problems are not for your professional participation or military solution. Your guidepost stands out like a ten-fold beacon in the night: Duty, Honor, Country.

This section marks the duty of the soldier first and foremost as one set apart for a definite task removed from other spheres of influence and responsibility. MacArthur's own life is a testament to those "controversial issues . . . which divide men's minds." Older members of his audience could afford a private smile in recognition of MacArthur's public battles with those outside his sphere of military responsibility. In the end, the solace MacArthur offers his cadets is the same solace in which he is finally forced to find refuge: the sanctity that separates civilian and military ways of life. Again and again and again MacArthur reminds his audience that that sanctity is the code itself: Duty, Honor, Country.

Conclusion: Stir of Echoes

The shadows are lengthening for me. The twilight is
here. My days of old have vanished, tone and tint.
They have gone glimmering through the dreams of
things that were. Their memory is one of wondrous
beauty, watered by tears, and coaxed and caressed
by the smiles of yesterday. I listen vainly, but with
thirsty ears, for the witching melody of faint bugles
blowing reveille, of far drums beating the long roll. In
my dreams I hear again the crash of guns, the rattle
of musketry, the strange, mournful mutter of the
battlefield. But in the evening of my memory, always I
come back to West Point. Always there echoes and
re-echoes: Duty, Honor, Country.

MacArthur's eloquent opening to his conclusion is brief
but poignant. Over the course of the speech he has offered
his audience an array of images to convey the emotional
resonance of the code. In this section he bares his heart
openly in rueful reminiscing. Unstated but perhaps deeply
felt is the sentiment presented to the young cadets in his
audience that they have their whole lives ahead of them
and that those lives must be living testimonies to the code
of honor. More than that, MacArthur is passing along the
code's romance. It is a code to be cherished and loved and
only in that will its honor truly be found in them. It is an
entirely moving and convincing treatment of a code whose
ultimate purpose must necessarily transcend individual
human experience even as it is embodied by each individual soldier. The code's romance offers MacArthur one
last unspoken word to the young cadets: "I envy you for

the battles for which you will fight, for the honor you will receive, and for the duty in which you will persevere."

Rhetorical Impact

Eyewitness accounts of the event claim that there was not a dry eye in the place. Battle-hardened officers together with bright-eyed cadets felt deeply the force of MacArthur's rhetoric. That force was made possible through the way in which the content of his speech was wedded to its structure. MacArthur navigated the microstructural requirements of the introduction, establishing rapport, previewing his content, and establishing the speaker's relationship to the topic at hand. In establishing rapport, MacArthur began with a tone of levity that provided an ironic point of departure for the emotional depth of the rest of his speech. Within the topical arrangement of the body, MacArthur progressed logically from the meaning and value of the award itself as embodied within a code of chivalry to honor and duty of a soldier. Finally, in the conclusion, briefly stated, MacArthur did not summarize his previous material, but chose instead to mark its significance through self-reflection on a life lived in service to the code.

I've moved quickly and rather dryly through the summary of MacArthur's speech because there is a larger point I would like to make about the nature of acceptance speeches per se. By contemporary standards, perhaps the most remarkable aspect of MacArthur's acceptance lies in the fact that it is utterly devoid of the single most frequently occurring phrase in modern acceptance addresses. This is a *good* thing, for the words "thank you" are really shorthanded, unsatisfying responses to important obligations that every speaker has when delivering a public acceptance. And multiplying the words a few, or even a dozen, times over—as modeled by countless Hollywood acceptance award speeches—does not make matters any better for the speaker or for the audience. It merely repeats the "sin" of failing to meet one's rhetorical obligations that many more times over.

I use *sin* loosely here, but it is apt in a moral sense in that the best acceptance addresses on record, dating back to classical times, really amount to a kind of confessional on the part of the speaker. And you don't have to be Catholic to realize that coming clean is more than just saying, "I'm sorry." It has a recounting of things for which one is sorry and is usually combined with a recognition of the severity of their implications and a promise to change one's behavior. The confessional status of an acceptance address is that of deeply felt gratitude, expressed in words and images that explain why the speaker is thankful, what the award means to him or her personally, and what the award means for the larger community from which it issues. Both the audience and the award are owed at least this much. "Thank you" is, by comparison, a rather cheap substitute for what the audience truly deserves. Meeting confessional obligations in this way is, in the final analysis, an expression of love for the audience; the kind of love that values the best in them emotionally, intellectually, spiritually. These were the ultimate values that animated MacArthur's acceptance, making it not only a grand exit but a personal confession of deeply felt gratitude and an eloquent expression of how to love one's audience.

5

Style

John F. Kennedy's Inaugural Address

ON JANUARY 21, 1961, at 12:00 P.M. (EST), President John
F. Kennedy delivered his inaugural address to an immediate audience of several thousand and a national radio
and television audience of some forty million. Delivered in
just less than fourteen minutes, it was the fourth-shortest
presidential inaugural address on record. It is also widely
considered to be not only the finest inaugural address but
also the finest speech delivered in the twentieth century by
an American politician.

John Fitzgerald Kennedy

John Fitzgerald Kennedy (May 29, 1917–November 22,
1963) was born in Brookline, Massachusetts, the second
of four sons of Joseph and Rose Kennedy. The elder Joseph
Kennedy, a business tycoon and influential powerbroker
within the Democratic Party, had tapped his eldest son,
Joseph Patrick, for political success leading to the U.S.

presidency. When Joseph Jr. was tragically killed in 1944 when his B-24 bomber, overladen with explosives, blew up over Blythburgh, England, the mantle of the Kennedy family's political ambitions fell squarely on the shoulders of John Fitzgerald.

Blessed with prepossessing charm and natural inquisitiveness, John F. Kennedy graduated from preparatory school in 1935 where he was named "Most likely to become President." Kennedy graduated with honors from Harvard University in 1940 and entered military service with the U.S. Navy. His naval service was punctuated by the *PT-109* incident in which he was awarded the Navy and Marine Corps Medal for "outstanding courage, endurance and leadership courageous" efforts in saving the lives of several crew members after their ship had been destroyed by a Japanese destroyer. Kennedy also earned a Purple Heart.

Kennedy was elected to the United States House of Representatives in 1946 where he served three terms. He was elected to the U.S. Senate in 1952. In a refreshingly terse announcement in 1960, Kennedy announced his candidacy for the U.S. presidency. One issue that gained traction concerned Kennedy's Catholic faith and how that faith might influence his political decisions as president. Appearing before a group of Protestant ministers in Houston, Kennedy delivered a speech followed by a series of extemporaneous remarks during a direct question-and-answer session from the audience that successfully navigated a course between a defense of his religious faith as "personal" and an attack on those who would use it to challenge his ability to meet his "public" duties as president. Emblematic of Kennedy's style was the consciously styled message of tolerance—not unlike that of Edward Kennedy's address at Liberty Baptist College—in which the perceptions were gently shifted from Kennedy the "Catholic American" to Kennedy the "American Catholic."

In a closely contested race for the Democratic nomination, Kennedy defeated political rivals Senator Hubert Humphrey of Minnesota and Senator Lyndon B. Johnson of Texas, whom he later asked to be his vice president in an effort to gain support from southern constituents of the Democratic Party.

With the Democratic Party nomination secured, Kennedy turned his sights on the Republican Party nominee for president and current vice president Richard Nixon. In a series of debates broadcast on radio and television, voter judgment was apparently swayed by the medium of exposure. Nixon was given more favorable reviews by those who listened on the radio, while many voters watching the debates on television found Nixon's comparatively stiff, stubble-faced image overmatched by Kennedy's youthful looks, polished stage presence, and ingratiating style of speech. Kennedy won the election by one of the closest margins of victory ever and in 1960 became the youngest person and the first Catholic elected to the U.S. presidency.

Theory of Style

The content of a speech, like the human body, must be clothed appropriately to fit the occasion, audience, speaker, and purpose(s). The *style* of a speech refers to the linguistic manner in which ideas are "fitted" or expressed. There are several dimensions to rhetorical style in public speaking, ranging from figures of expression, such as *metaphor* and *antithesis* to considerations of the relative "level of abstraction" in which ideas may be more and less readily understood. Considerations of style extend also to mundane matters of grammar and syntax, although of the latter you will doubtless be happy to learn that little will be said as a matter of theory. Since Kennedy's inaugural address is rich in rhetorical figures and strategic abstractions, and since his style contributed a great deal not only to its immediate import—Cuban dictator Fidel Castro was so moved by its eloquence that he immediately and entirely uncharacteristically declared, not offered, a treaty of peace with the United States—but to its lasting fame, we must pause to consider the *concept* of style before turning to Kennedy's particularly effective use of it.

Consider the amiable beggars who inhabit the corners and walkways just south of downtown New Orleans who have developed well-honed figures of speech to relieve passersby of whatever money is left after the rest of the Quarter has had its way with them. "Cold night, warm heart" is one such expression. In the face of such economy of style, I froze. There, within a stream of four one-syllable words, an ocean of meaning and sentiment foamed up and overwhelmed my usually guarded rational faculties. Had my wits not been so entirely disarmed, I might have responded with something like "Deep heart, shallow pockets" but I didn't—I couldn't.

You may dismiss this episode as the overly sensitive response of a naive traveler to the Crescent City, and you may well be right. But the truth is, each of us has been or likely will be humbled at some point after hearing some particularly disarming phrase that gets to us in spite of our pretensions to be "rhetoric proof." Indeed, the expression "mere rhetoric" captures the suspicion that many feel when listening to a speech whose style seems not only self-possessed but out of all proportion to the substance or content it conveys. "Give me plain talk or no talk at all."

And therein lies the rub. The truth is, even our sentiments in favor of "plain talk" invoke certain, if not consciously realized, figures of expression. Most content that we remember, and even cherish, has been styled in a way calculated to evoke those feelings.

Figures of style grant content an appearance it would not otherwise possess. That appearance may be one of simplicity or of sophistication. It may sweeten or sour our disposition toward an idea; it may quicken or lengthen the mind's ability to comprehend and even retain ideas.

The style of the best speeches is to substance as beauty is to truth. Style is both a source of attraction in its own right and an important influence on whether and to what extent we consume content. The allure of an attractive style often makes it easier to attend to content, particularly when its truth is hard, even cold.

At a more concrete level, there are a few particularly prominent figures of expression worth identifying. Most readers will readily recognize the figures *metaphor* and *simile*. Less readily recognized is the fact that these figures of comparison do more than merely "fluff" an idea. They invite us to participate in new perspectives on an idea that content alone cannot produce. The concept of social justice in Martin Luther King Jr.'s I Have a Dream speech would remain rather dry, even ethereal, were it not given a "palace" in which to reign, bestowed with the power of Mother Nature to "roll down like waters" whose currents come to rest in an "oasis" of peaceful equality. King understood the power of style to modify human perception, and the power of his "dream" flowed from a steady stream of metaphors and similes that gave fresh rhetorical life to a vision as old as the U.S. Constitution.

Antithesis, a favorite figure of Kennedy's, presents opposing ideas in adjacent clauses and phrases. Well used, the effect is jolting, playing upon the mind's healthy bipolar tendency to make sense of one thing in terms of an opposite. "Light" makes sense because of "darkness." "Hot" makes sense because of "cold." Abraham Lincoln's Gettysburg Address, one of the greatest speeches of any genre ever delivered on American soil, contains several instances of effective antithesis, but none more memorable than "The world will little note nor long remember what we say here; but it can never forget what they did here." The juxtaposition of "nor long remember" with "never forget" and "what we say here" with "what they did here" solemnizes the idea of dutiful remembrance for deeds well done for a noble cause far more memorably and eloquently than, well, "dutiful remembrance for deeds well done for a noble cause." The antithesis invites cognitive attention and forces the mind to make sense of the idea in opposing terms that command allegiance: if you don't remember what I say, "thou shalt remember what they did." As history records, the command was only partially heeded: We remember both what Lincoln said and the noble deeds he noted.

Often, though not necessarily, antithesis is accompanied by *parallelism*, a syntactically balanced string of phrases or clauses. "Loving well" while "having fun" and "living life" is one such string. Another appears in what is arguably the most important American political address delivered thus far in the twenty-first century: "We've seen the unfurling of flags, the lighting of candles, the giving of blood, the saying of prayers." George W. Bush's September 20, 2001, address to a joint session of Congress and the American people is proof enough that parallelism is neither the province of a particular political party (*alliteration*) nor the exclusive property of or indentured servant (*allusion*) to the rhetorically gifted.

You probably noticed the two additional figures. If this is the first time you have experienced alliteration, there is something missing in your life and I will leave you to find out about it on your own terms. The second figure deserves sustained and special attention in view of Kennedy's particular rhetorical habit of quoting from his elders.

Owing to a love of literature, but due also to an express desire to be remembered as an erudite speaker, Kennedy was given to quoting lines from great literary works, whether paraphrased or verbatim. Literary quotations are one among several kinds of allusion, a figure of amplification that connects a present moment in a speech to some notable and typically well-known person, place, thing, event, or statement situated in the past. Allusions employ indirect means of amplification in that key missing points of connection are left to the audience to find and fill in. For example, recently, when a mother heard that her bashful and unmotivated son had made the six o'clock news, she retorted with "Yes, well, everyone gets their fifteen minutes." She alluded to Andy Warhol's statement that everyone will have fifteen minutes of fame, to amplify her convictions about her son's apparent laziness. At the very least, audiences would need to add the words "of fame" to make sense of things, even if the broader connection to the mass media's influence on pop culture and the implications for all of us are beyond the sense-making capacity of this mother.

Among the various figures of speech Kennedy enjoyed using throughout an all-too-brief rhetorical career, perhaps none rings forth with more raw rhetorical charm than the unfortunately named *antimetabole* (ant-ee-met-AB-oh-lee). Don't let the name fool you. This is one sexy beast of a figure that curries favor with deceptive simplicity by reversing the order of words across successive clauses and phrases. George Bernard Shaw's "We do not stop playing because we grow old; we grow old because we stop playing" and former United Nations Secretary-General Kofi Annan's "There can be no security without development and no development without security" testify to the figure's power to make playful ideas even more fun to play with and to transform tentative infrastructural truisms into strikingly self-assured nation-builders.

Unlike either antithesis or parallelism, Kennedy's fondness for this figure is evidenced not by a quantity of appearance but by a quality of implementation. A number of Kennedy's most important addresses feature one or at most two antimetaboles, and always in the company of the most important of ideas. In a Houston, Texas, campaign address designed chiefly to quell suspicions about the role his Catholic faith would play in the Oval Office, Kennedy's most decisively executed line to an audience of Protestant ministers ran, "I believe in a President whose views on religion are his own private affair, neither imposed upon him by the nation, nor imposed by the nation upon him as a condition to holding that office." In an important address to the United Nations following the untimely death of its secretary-general, Dag Hammarskjöld, Kennedy trumpeted that body's critical function in world affairs with, "Mankind must put an end to war or war will put an end to mankind." Many other instances may be found in kind. As one reserves fine china for the most special occasions and in only the most select company, so Kennedy used his beloved antimetabole.

The list of figures does exhaust our education, but we have other promises to keep and miles to go before ———. Interested readers may go to AmericanRhetoric.com's "Figures of Speech" section and find many more figures than are discussed in this book. Besides, if you were able to name the rhetorical figure presented—and summarily cut short—in the opening sentence of this paragraph, you may consider yourself good to go on general stylistic grounds. This section was designed as an introduction to a few of the more important figures of speech as well as to cultivate some appreciation for the privileged place that rhetorical style enjoys in the constitution of great oratory.

As we learned in Chapter 2, great oratory often occurs within the context of pressing circumstances that give rise to a rhetorical situation. Missing from that discussion is the realization that some kinds of speeches, such as inaugural addresses, are also driven by generic conventions of the occasion. This is why, for instance, Kennedy's inaugural could invoke "God" several times over without raising anew the suspicions of his religious inquisitors in Houston. The generic conventions of the inaugural serve to defend the choice to include "God" on stylistic grounds, given the historical norms of the occasion. To further appreciate these norms we turn to briefly consider the role that context plays in the shaping of this particular address.

A Celebration of Democracy: The Inaugural Address

Presidential inaugural ceremonies are celebrations of democracy. After the polls have closed and the votes tallied and democracy thereby preserved, it must now be performed.

Principal players representing the various branches of government have prescribed, traditional roles in the inaugural ceremony. The judicial branch, represented by the chief justice, is given the constitutional role of administering the oath of office to the chief executive. The legislative branch is well accounted for in the many senators and leaders in the House of Representatives given prominent platform seating behind the podium and who lend to the entire event an elevated air of political importance. The starring role is given to the newly elected (or reelected) chief executive, who in that role is also granted the best lines. The principal event of the presidential inaugural ceremony is the inaugural address.

If there be any truth in the saying "to all things a season," that truth surely is meted out in the inaugural address. The tendentious and even vituperative rhetoric of the presidential primaries and national conventions gives way to the ceremoniously ingratiating tones of the inaugural address. A "time to fight" gives way to a "time to heal." Continuity and change are the most dominant motifs coursing through the inaugural speech, with due emphasis given to one or the other depending upon whether the newly elected president is beginning a first or second term.

In passing, it is worth noting that although the style of the inaugural benefited from a number of comments and suggestions enlisted from trusted speechwriters, as well as from previous addresses delivered by Kennedy himself, it was the stylistic contributions of Ted Sorensen that produced some of the more memorable lines. Sorensen had been given the title of "alter ego" to Kennedy in view of his well-documented capacity for capturing Kennedy's ideas in that endearingly lyrical economy of style most favored by Kennedy.

That inaugural ceremonies and addresses are marked by convention should not distract us from the often interesting collision of interests that mark a given inaugural address. The host of political dignitaries dressed in overcoats and top hats and seated in armchairs nearest the podium included Vice President Johnson, with whom Kennedy shared a necessarily pragmatic political relationship but little else; defeated GOP presidential candidate and former vice president Richard Nixon; and immediate past president Dwight D. Eisenhower. Also present was Kennedy's father, Joseph Kennedy Sr., whose behind-the-scenes political dealings on behalf of his son were probably as much responsible for his son's successful presidential campaign as any one person could be. The wives of the principals were given platform seating as well.

The day's bright winter sun's piercing rays were betrayed by a sharp winter chill, a stark reminder that the temperature at inaugural time was well below freezing. Thurston Clarke's definitive account of Kennedy's inaugural address, *Ask Not*, reveals that Kennedy chose to wear long underwear so he could remove his overcoat when he addressed his audiences in order to cultivate a persona of health and youthful vigor. Amphetamine prescriptions and two steroid injections—long used by Kennedy to help control various health problems—also helped to assure that the benefits of human science would control the climactic conditions stipulated by Mother Nature on this particular rhetorical occasion.

Robert Frost, a favorite poet of Kennedy's, opened the inaugural ceremony with a poem composed specifically for the occasion. Chief Justice Earl Warren, who, in two years, ten months, and three days would serve as Kennedy's chief eulogist and subsequently chief commissioner of the body charged with the formal investigation of Kennedy's assassination, dictated the oath of office, as specified in Article II, Section 1 of the U.S. Constitution. Oddly enough, given Kennedy's abundant experience delivering public speeches, the inaugural address was the beneficiary of months of private (i.e., secret) coaching in which substantial attention was apparently devoted both to verbal (pacing, pausing, and inflection) and nonverbal (eye contact, body posture, and movement) dimensions of delivery.

Then, in a brief fourteen minutes, John F. Kennedy gave the address that captivated the world.

A Remarkable Lightness of Being

Broadly considered, the most striking impression one gets from the inaugural lies in its remarkable lightness of being. Political party pettiness, the onslaught of powerful new military-industrial technologies, global poverty, the ever-present threat of war, the growing complexities of daily life, and the sheer weight of responsibility given to the citizens and leaders of the most powerful nation in recorded history—the gravity of any one of these alone is potentially enough to exhaust any and all efforts at sustained attention, let alone offer an incentive for marked enthusiasm. And yet those ideas, each taken up in turn and so styled, not only lighten our burden but become positively gravity-defying sources of energy. Of course, in matters of style it is the little rhetorical things that add up to the big rhetorical effects and to those things we must primarily look.

We observe today not a victory of party, but a celebration of freedom—symbolizing an end, as well

as a beginning—signifying renewal, as well as change.
For I have sworn before you and Almighty God the
same solemn oath our forebears prescribed nearly a
century and three-quarters ago.

Immediately out of the gate, Kennedy opens with a series
of antitheses in parallel balance. The first antithesis is
both relatively loose and double-decked with "victory/
party" offset by "celebration/freedom." In addition, the
latter terms, "celebration" and "freedom," are strategically
broad in scope so as to capture the ideologically higher and
more inclusive ground. That is to say, that "celebration"
is broader than "victory," and "freedom" is broader than
"party." The second and third antitheses are starkly configured by comparison, juxtaposing "end" with "beginning"
and "renewal" with "change" but in a way that preserves
the dignity of both.

Not to be missed is the subtle but insistent use of alliteration in the form of the "s" sound that courses through
the entire section in such words as "celebration," "symbolizing," "signifying," "sworn," and "same solemn." It is,
as such, an attention-grabbing device that together with
antithesis and parallelism, signify to the audience that
there will be no style-free warming up phase for the audience. We should also note the invocation of "God." Consistent with his purposeful decisive style, Kennedy signifies
to his audience that he is comfortable with religious ter-
minology—again right out of the gate—even, perhaps, in
somewhat open defiance of those who made his Catholic
faith an issue during the campaign. It would be difficult
not to imagine at least some of those Protestant ministers
he had addressed just a few months earlier wincing a bit
at the obvious confident ease with which Kennedy invokes

God—and so early on. With these stylistic attributes, Kennedy's speech has hit the ground running, purpose-driven and unabashed.

> *The world is very different now. For man holds in his mortal hands the power to abolish all forms of human poverty and all forms of human life. And yet the same revolutionary beliefs for which our forebears fought are still at issue around the globe—the belief that the rights of man come not from the generosity of the state, but from the hand of God.*

Those acquainted with different kinds of alliteration will note with "holds . . . hands" and "forebears fought," both non-immediate and immediate forms, now forges Kennedy's alliterative pace. But there is bigger stylistic news. Here, as promised, is our first "discovery" of an as-of-yet unidentified rhetorical figure. *Anaphora*, perhaps the most frequently used—I do not say the greatest—rhetorical figure of all time, occurs when the first word or set of words is or are repeated across successive phrases or clauses. Often, the figure is most often used for emphasis, as Mario Cuomo's 1984 Democratic National Convention address illustrates: "The Republicans believe that the wagon train will not make it to the frontier unless some of the old, some of the young, some of the weak are left behind by the side of trail." The phrase "some of the" is hardly provocative on its face. Styled in the form of anaphora, however, it quickly seizes our immediate attention—and this is a relatively innocuous use of the figure.

Far more aggressive forms occur in various stock political declarations such as "I believe in an America that . . ." and "I believe in an America that . . ." where what follows is given additional significance precisely because of its connection to the repeated phrase before it. Perhaps most important, the anaphora conditions us to expect certain things from what next occurs. After hearing "I believe in an America that" several times followed by a positively patriotic idea, we expect that the next "I believe" statement in the sequence will be succeeded by yet another positively stated patriotic idea.

Given this understanding, it is clear that Kennedy's "all forms of human" is an instance of anaphora. But it is not a typical instance. There is a twist. The first phrase puts a positive spin on the normally negative term "poverty." Conditioned by the positive spin, we expect the second phrase to follow a similarly positive path up to and even including the term "human." Only after, albeit very quickly after, the phrase is delivered in its entirety does its effect move beyond our mere sense of hearing into the higher cognitive processing functions of the mind and we feel the anaphora's full force. The first part takes a normally negative term in "poverty" and with "abolish" places it within a positive context. The second part takes a normally positive term in "human life" and also with "abolish" spins it negatively. The effect is jolting and, occurring so early in the inaugural, that the effect is not likely to be forgotten, even if the content itself is. This will not be the first time Kennedy's style will play tricks on the senses and sensibilities of his audiences.

And there is a lesson here. At a substantive level Kennedy has styled the ever-objective, data-collecting, hypothesis-driven, theory-building enterprise of "science" itself in starkly disquietingly moral terms. Science can be good. Science can be bad. But science cannot be morally neutral. However, science is not the only entity to be so styled. Kennedy's audience is also being styled as citizen-participants in an increasingly sophisticated society in which technological progress and moral responsibility must travel hand in hand, or not travel at all. That is, this is perhaps the first audience of its generation to have to come to terms with the changing dynamic of personal identity, one which must become comfortable with rapid technological advancement born of the intellect, without reducing the personal importance of nurturing the individual human spirit. Of course, when matters move over into the spiritual, questions about "God" come to the fore. And thanks to Kennedy, "God" enjoys a privileged place with this most hallowed of political-ceremonial stages.

Lest his hearers think they had imagined hearing about "God," Kennedy removes all doubt by offering up "God" again, this time juxtaposed with the interests of the state. At one level, this is an obvious gesture against the ideology of communism, one which would invert the relationship between church and state by claiming "our rights come not from the hand of God but from the generosity of the state." At a second level, the close semantic quarters between "state" and "God"—separated by only five words within the same sentence—suggests a relationship by analogy: even as sharp lines of division must be drawn between church and state, the two institutions must cooperate to coexist in a state of mutually assured construction.

> *Let the word go forth from this time and place, to*
> *friend and foe alike, that the torch has been passed to*
> *a new generation of Americans—born in this century,*
> *tempered by war, disciplined by a hard and bitter*
> *peace, proud of our ancient heritage, and unwilling*
> *to witness or permit the slow undoing of those human*

rights to which this nation has always been committed,
and to which we are committed today at home and
around the world.

Kennedy's styling of his audience continues with increasing urgency fostered by variations in alliteration and parallelism. The combinations of "forth from," "friend and foe," and "peace, proud . . . permit" continue to press the alliterative pace forged at the outset. This section contains Kennedy's most strident attempt yet to style his audience as a "new generation," and he does it with the full force of metaphor rhetorically bonded with allusion. The metaphor compares the passing of a "torch" with collections of people living in two different periods in time. The metaphor's power is wrought in the idea that people separated by time are nonetheless united in purpose, and that purpose is itself eternally re-energized through the image of liberty's eternally burning flame. The metaphor thus creates an idea about liberty as a responsible process given from one generation to another and invests that idea with particular emotional force that is deeply woven into the hearts of every American—the emotionally compelling force of liberty and freedom that is our national heritage.

As to allusion, "The torch has been passed" readily calls to mind the Olympic relay runner who must take up the cause anew—and rightly so, because for that runner it is new. That cause, like the relay race, cannot be accomplished in the absence of what has gone on before. Indeed, it can only be participated in because of what has already been accomplished. But neither can that cause be advanced by dwelling on the successes and failures of the past. By these stylistic means, Kennedy's figurative devices conspire together to fashion an overwhelmingly persuasive tone of positive progress, and it is a race that the "new generation" has been called to run.

Olympic relay races are not run by a single team. They are run by many teams from different nations who compete together. Thus, the allusion provides a point of entry for Kennedy to take up specifically the subject of what we face in the competing forces of other nations, both friendly and hostile.

> *Let every nation know, whether it wishes us well or ill, that we shall pay any price, bear any burden, meet any hardship, support any friend, oppose any foe, to assure the survival and the success of liberty.*

Again, we find Kennedy pressing alliteration's stylistic cause with "whether . . . wishes . . . well," "pay . . . price," "bear . . . burden," and "survival . . . success." We find also in this textual moment a very confidently balanced use of parallelism. Actually, that is an understatement. The first five parallel sequences, beginning with "pay any price" are *perfectly* balanced, syntactically (parts of speech), semantically (number of words), and syllabically (five per phrase). Barbara Jordan once commented that linguistic consistency is a sign of moral consistency. I don't know about that—and I'm not sure what to make of it in light of Kennedy's own sense of morality—but we might add that perfect linguistic symmetry presents a very convincing appearance of moral decisiveness. If Kennedy's opponents in hostile countries were considering the prospect of testing his moral resolve, they surely could not have been encouraged by such symmetrical decisiveness.

Space considerations mandate that I move further forward in the speech. But you need not, necessarily. You have enough knowledge to capably mine the next several paragraphs of the speech with little need of further help. I might mention just a few of the obvious places where Kennedy's figures present themselves. Doubtless, you will note the growing presence of metaphors. In your excursion, you will find family friendly metaphors ("sister republics") and hostile metaphors of organic ("prey of hostile powers") and inorganic ("chains of poverty") composition. You will likely note the pervasive use of extended anaphoras beginning with "to" and "to those" used by Kennedy to first identify and then address the economic and security concerns of audiences listening in different parts of the world. You will also note the anaphoric construction that finds Kennedy at his most emotionally impassioned as he details our various calls to moral duty beginning with the invitationally styled "Let both sides . . ." The net effect provides additional evidence as to how this particular figure of emphasis creates and inspires decisive confidence.

Other notable instances of antithesis, parallelism, alliteration, metaphor, simile, and allusion abound. With respect to the latter figure, see if you can determine what Kennedy meant by "Those who foolishly sought power by riding the back of the tiger ended up inside." Recall that allusions only work if the audience has enough knowledge to fill in the gaps of missing information. As you move through this line in your audio, listen carefully to the audience's response. If you listen very carefully you will hear at least one person laugh aloud. It is the first—and to my ears only—time that Kennedy's speech elicited overt laughter. This is oddly noteworthy because the story on which it is based is not particularly funny. But it sure could be taken that way in the absence of the story's original context and meaning.

At any rate, a final matter of style await us in the identification of Kennedy's most privileged figure of all, the
one he brought out on the most important of occasions
and used in the most significant of places in a speech on
those occasions.

> *But neither can two great and powerful groups of*
> *nations take comfort from our present course—both*
> *sides overburdened by the cost of modern weapons,*
> *both rightly alarmed by the steady spread of the deadly*
> *atom, yet both racing to alter that uncertain balance*
> *of terror that stays the hand of mankind's final war.*
> *So let us begin anew—remembering on both sides*
> *that civility is not a sign of weakness, and sincerity is*
> *always subject to proof. Let us never negotiate out of*
> *fear, but let us never fear to negotiate.*

Among the various figures of style—that include antithesis
and alliteration—in this section there is one that stands
apart from them all. All the more so, if you listen to the
speech at the same time. We have in "Let us never negotiate . . ." Kennedy's first of only two instances of antimetabole. It is used to bring emotional finality to the litany
of holy horrors that preceded it in "the economic burden
borne of the atomic military monster that both the U.S.
and the U.S.S.R. were feeding without hope of any end in
sight save for the end of all humankind." The figure also
begins the next section in which Kennedy sets forth a positive agenda for the hope of a lasting peace. The figure thus
stands in the gap, separating the two trajectories and in
that gap beckons both sides to end their enmity by resist-
ing their very common enemy: fear.

Kennedy uses the figure only once more some moments later in what has passed into history as not only the most readily identifiable line of this particular address but quite possibly the most readily identified line in a political address of any kind since the advent of modern broadcasting and recording technologies.

To be sure, other great speakers and speeches have had their rhetorical moments in the sun. Franklin Delano Roosevelt's first inaugural address had hardly gotten out of its own gate when the words "let me assert my firm belief that the only thing we have to fear is fear itself" rang out with astonishing starkness. Considered rhetorically, it was the beginning of the end of the Great Depression. For although the Depression raged for years, the people's trust in Roosevelt and, more important, in themselves grew.

Barbara Jordan, whose remarks at the Nixon impeachment hearings we cover next in Chapter 6 on delivery, may well have delivered the singly most important line in any political convention of the twentieth century with the seemingly innocuous: "I, Barbara Jordan, and keynote speaker . . ." It was the first time in the history of our nation that an African-American woman had addressed a convention of any political party as a keynote speaker. Her line, coming nearly two hundred years to the day after the Declaration of Independence, was the embodiment of two hundred years of equality for all in the making. It was an astoundingly powerful rhetorical moment.

Much later, Ronald Reagan would call out then Soviet leader Mikhail Gorbachev with a statement that, if it did not cause, most certainly signified the most singularly revolutionary political event of the latter half of the twentieth century: "General Secretary Gorbachev, if you seek peace, if you seek prosperity for the Soviet Union and Eastern Europe . . . tear down this wall!"

There are other lines, of course, that could be—perhaps even should be!—included in such a list, each carrying singular importance on its own terms and within its own rhetorical context. But, it must be admitted, that none combine a singular significance in content with the sheer sublime force of eloquence given to Kennedy's arresting antimetabole: *And so, my fellow Americans, ask not what your country can do for you; ask what you can do for your country.*

This is one of those lines that after you hear it a sufficient number of times, you cannot capture its content without citing the line exactly as it was figured. Somehow, "Serve your country selflessly!" "America: love it or leave it!" or any number of other stylistic prospects for capturing the same idea, including those less calculatingly trite, could not match the force of style granted Kennedy's antimetabole. I am reminded of the New Testament story of Jesus performing the first of his many miracles by turning water into wine. And, along with the astonished witness to the miracle, I am tempted to say, "You [Kennedy] have saved the best [l]ine until now."

Style Does Matter

This chapter's observations on and conclusions about the role and influence of style in the rhetorical process are at best tentatively offered. My overly enthusiastic convictions about style are partly a product of being too easily carried away by stylistic concerns generally, partly the product of Kennedy's inaugural eloquence in particular—more than a few presidential inaugurals have been, by comparison, exceptionally poorly conceived—and also a function of my appreciation for speeches that actually do bear witness to how important our language choices and devices are.

I'm hardly alone, at least with respect to Kennedy's inaugural. And I'm not talking about the company of fellow laborers in speechmaking per se. A cadre of rabbis in New York was so struck by the inaugural's eloquence that they audibly and openly hailed the dawn of a "great new era in world history." Understandably, President Eamon de Valera of Ireland praised Kennedy's tone as representational of Ireland's best rhetorical tradition. Less anticipated were the positive musings of the Chinese press who had only days earlier been highly critical of Kennedy's candidacy. Egyptian presses liked Kennedy's "fine words," a sentiment echoed throughout Latin America and extended even to Cuba, where Fidel Castro openly declared a treaty of peace with the United States. Detractors in the United States on either side of the aisle were hardly less laudatory of the eloquently pitched notes struck by Kennedy. Style does matter.

We have seen how variations in some figures, a dash of additional alliteration here, several strokes of confident parallelism and boisterous antithesis there, can greatly influence how we perceive the content of a speech. The style of Kennedy's speech produced a measure of a freshly paced, confident optimism that refused to be weighed down in the face of very real foreign and domestic burdens. In the end perhaps it is that style that helps to account for how Kennedy's inaugural achieved its entirely bearable lightness of being.

6

Delivery

Barbara Jordan's Statement on the Articles of Impeachment

ON JULY 25, 1974, the thundering tones emanating from Texan congresswoman Barbara Jordan proved to be the tipping point in the Watergate inquiry. Her "godlike" delivery was the necessary complement to her logical conclusion that the constitutional bar for impeachment had been reached.

Barbara Jordan

Barbara Charline Jordan (February 21, 1936–January 17, 1996) was born in Houston's Fifth Ward, a predominantly black, poverty-stricken urban section in the northeastern part of the city. Her father, Benjamin, was a Baptist minister. Jordan's mother, Arlyne, was also an orator of some repute within her church. Both parents were strong influences in their daughter's education and later oratorical experiences.

Jordan attended Phillis Wheatley High School where she excelled in debate and public speaking contests sponsored by Texas's University Interscholastic League (UIL), a statewide program designed to foster responsible citizenship among the state's youth.

It was also in high school that Jordan was introduced to a peculiar kind of racism. Wheatley's students were black, but not equally black. Color-struck teachers tended to favor lighter skinned students both in the classroom and with vocational and higher educational opportunities. By these measures, Jordan was, by degrees, too dark. She was also, by her own admission, too tall, too indelicately proportioned, too loud-spoken, too self-assured, too strong-willed, too intelligent, and far too competitive. Motivated by her parents, she set her sights on the most appropriate next step for someone so endowed: college.

Jordan enrolled at Texas Southern University, an all-black institution, where she channeled her natural gifts into a successful collegiate debate career. One memorable episode recalls an "unofficial" visit from perennial collegiate debating power Harvard University, whose members came to Texas Southern for the express purpose of debating Jordan and her debate partner. The contest ended in an unlikely tie, which Jordan considered, with typical bravado, a win.

Invigorated by her success in college, Jordan applied and was accepted to the prestigious law school at Boston University. For all her collegiate success, Jordan was ill-prepared for the level of intellectual rigor that the study of law required. Added to this was a large number of students in her class, all of whom were at least as intelligent and competitive as Jordan. Following her first semester of exams, she faced the very real prospect of failing.

She didn't. Jordan's overall score of 79, relatively unremarkable particularly by her own standards, was sufficiently encouraging to see her through the first year. Law school was a whole new approach to thinking for Jordan, involving an analytic thought process for which sheer determination and confidence alone would not be enough. Eventually, incrementally, painfully, Jordan's perseverance paid off and she earned her law degree.

With her oratorical prowess and newly minted powers of analysis, Jordan eventually entered into politics professionally, establishing a list of achievements that is astounding by any reasonable measure. In 1966, she became the first black woman elected to the Texas Senate. In 1972, she was the first black woman from the South elected to the U.S. House of Representatives and, with support from Lyndon Johnson, the first black woman to serve on the House Judiciary Committee. Later, on the strength of her speech delivered here, she delivered what is widely regarded as the finest convention keynote address in the last hundred years. Not surprisingly, she was the first black woman to deliver a Democratic National Convention keynote address, a speech that ranks among the top ten political speeches of the twentieth century and quite possibly the finest political convention address yet delivered by a woman. In 1995, less than a year before she passed away, Jordan became the first black woman to be awarded the Sylvanus Thayer Award.

Theory of Delivery

Legend has it that when the great Athenian orator-statesman Demosthenes was asked to identify the most important part of public speaking, he replied, "Delivery." His inquisitor, unsatisfied with such a Spartan response, pressed Demosthenes for further detail, to which Demosthenes further replied: "Delivery, delivery, delivery."

The story may or may not be true but it is suggestive of just how important delivery is in the process of public speaking. I suppose in one sense that saying delivery is the most important aspect of oratory is a bit like saying that the judicial branch is the most important branch of government. The judiciary only gets whatever importance may be imputed to its contribution to the effectiveness of American democracy because of and in concert with the other branches. That said, there is little doubting that a speaker's delivery is often that part of a speech where much of our critical and complimentary judgments about a speech as a whole most find their immediate source. Our forty-third president, for better and for worse, is a running YouTube icon for his delivery mannerisms. His consonant "s" often sounds like "sh" and, oddly enough, this is even more pronounced when a more than typical effort at articulation is made. And even where delivery is used as a point of cultural identity, as when "nuclear" gets "West Texafied" into "new-cue-lar"—although contrary to popular opinion, neither George W. Bush nor Texas are the only owners of this particular pronunciation—we do notice it and it does affect our perceptions of both speaker and message.

George W. Bush is hardly alone. Indeed, to be fair, we need only look to the address delivered by John Kerry at the 2004 Democratic National Convention for further evidence on the importance of delivery. Kerry's verbal stuttering, partly a result of the failure to negotiate audience reactions midstream, added at least ten minutes to an already too-long speech. When not stuttering, Kerry (mis)delivered such memorable lines as, "What does it mean when 25 percent of our children in Harlem have asthma because of *hair* pollution?" And, ". . . to strengthen American forces that are now overstretched, overextended, and under pressure, we will double our special forces to conduct *terrorist* operations" (emphases added). Kerry's speech delivery was ineffective enough in places to make his content seem positively incoherent. The point is, we notice delivery.

Given our attention to delivery it may come as some surprise that there is a comparatively scant body of theory in the field of speech communication devoted to it. American public speaking textbooks and manuals offer modestly specific recommendations on delivery in comparison with content, structure, and style.

True enough, the text of a speech is not the same as a score of music. The myriad of technical cues for delivery regulating matters of tempo, volume, pitch, and inflection make all the difference in the world in how music itself is interpreted. A change of rhythm here and a tempo modulation there transformed Beethoven's Fifth Symphony into a recipe for a hit song during the heyday of disco fever. There is no comparatively systematic treatment for regulating the ways in which verbal and nonverbal delivery might be manipulated to achieve various persuasive ends.

This was not always so. The elocutionary movement that flourished in eighteenth- and nineteenth-century England produced a remarkably rich body of thought on training and manipulating the human voice and body to help interpret and amplify content. It is easy enough to guess why the movement is no longer in vogue. At one point, the types and techniques for hand and facial gestures alone numbered in the hundreds! But this was not the primary problem. The movement faded in the wake of two withering facts about the relationship between delivery and public speaking.

First, the grandiose expressions used by speakers trained in the elocutionary style struck audiences of public speech as unnatural, even ridiculous. It turns out that a speech really wasn't made more effective by two robotically sweeping arm gestures and a facial twitch of almost monstrous proportions. And in a world where the "good speakers" had to be first and foremost good actors, the content of speeches was too easily reduced to playing a bit part, a vehicle by which one could display delivery prowess. Under such influence, the discipline of rhetoric itself was increasingly seen as an empty and puffed-up affair—full of sound and fury, perhaps, but little else.

Even more damaging to the elocutionists was the fact that some speeches, delivered by "untrained" speakers, were achieving powerful public results. Where frenetic delivery was used effectively, as it was with the circuit preachers in rural England and America, it was a natural and spontaneous, if less polished, outgrowth of the speaker's convictions about the content. And the delivery practices could vary widely. Consider the great religious speakers of the eighteenth century: Anglican priest George Whitefield's histrionics could whip a crowd into a religious frenzy within minutes. Yet, Jonathan Edwards's relatively subdued delivery was still powerful enough to arouse the religious convictions of several generations of Massachusetts congregants in the 1730s and '40s during what became known as the First Great Awakening.

That said, the art of delivery is something to take very seriously and to that end there are a few fundamentals worth noting. First, let's define some key terms. *Delivery* refers to the *verbal* and *nonverbal* means by which content is transmitted between speaker and audience. Verbal delivery refers to audible aspects of the human voice, including pitch, rate, volume, pace, tone, and smoothness. By smoothness I mean the absence of stuttering and other kinds of intonations such as "uh," "um," "you know," "you know what I'm sayin'," "like," and such. These intonations, important in keeping the flow moving during interpersonal and small group communication, tend to undermine not only content comprehension but also speaker credibility in public speaking situations.

Effective delivery contributes positively to our perceptions of speaker competence, confidence, knowledge, character, goodwill, and trustworthiness. Nonverbal delivery includes facial movements, hand gestures, and body posture and movement, essentially anything other than the human voice that shapes our perceptions of speaker and content.

We should also note several varieties of delivery, each having its strengths. *Memorized*, as the term suggests, refers to content that has been committed in whole or in part to memory. Very few public speakers memorize an entire speech, though important sections of a long speech may be memorized. A read, or *manuscript-based*, delivery refers to speeches whose content is entirely codified in writing. A careless or mistaken remark in a political or religious leader's public addresses can lead to dire consequences—even national conflict. To minimize that possibility, speeches are written out and read from a manuscript and/or teleprompter. *Extemporaneous* refers to delivery that is based on a working familiarity with the speech but which relies on an outline or set of notes. Extemporaneous delivery allows for greater flexibility in how the content is conveyed.

Finally, when a speaker has done very little to no preparation for a particular speech and uses very few if any notes, the delivery is called *impromptu*. Relatively few speeches born of significant rhetorical situations are delivered impromptu. However, situations that allow for a direct question-and-answer session following an address do provide the opportunity for impromptu remarks. One notable case is found in the question-and-answer session following John F. Kennedy's address to the Greater Houston Ministerial Association in September 1960. In that case, Kennedy was posed a number of hypothetical situations involving the relationship between church and state by clergy concerned over the extent to which his Roman Catholic faith would influence his presidential decisions. It was a watershed moment in Kennedy's campaign, and his impromptu responses, delivered with good-natured optimism, allayed much of his inquisitors' fears.

"We, the People": The House Judiciary Committee Impeachment Investigations

The Nixon Administration had been mired in the Watergate probe for nearly two years by the time the U.S. House Judiciary Committee began formal presidential impeachment investigations. What began with the grand jury indictment of five men on charges of burglary and wiretapping at the Democratic National Committee headquarters had escalated into a scandal of seismic proportions, implicating the CIA, the FBI, and the Department of Justice, as well as many of Nixon's senior-level advisors. In the spring of 1973, the U.S. Senate launched its own committee to investigate the Watergate break-in, which would eventually result in the formal indictment of some forty administration officials.

Prompted by the findings of the U.S. Senate and fueled by the investigative journalism of the *Washington Post* and the *New York Times*, the House of Representatives passed House Resolution 803 authorizing the Judiciary Committee "to investigate fully and completely whether sufficient grounds exist for the House of Representatives to exercise its constitutional power to impeach Richard M. Nixon, President of the United States of America."

The House Judiciary Committee convened in the spring of 1974 to consider impeachment proceedings pursuant to House Resolution 803. For the next five months the committee met in closed-door sessions to determine whether impeachment proceedings were warranted. Jordan remained publicly silent during this time. Behind the scenes she consulted ranking members of Congress, prior impeachment cases at varying levels of government, writings and statements by the constitutional fathers, and the U.S. Constitution itself to help interpret the various impeachment criteria.

Over time, Jordan came to the conviction that Nixon's actions constituted knowing and willing impeachable breaches of his executive authority. Most of her colleagues, however, were not convinced, and Jordan's initial efforts at trying to persuade them to vote immediately on the issue of impeachment were unsuccessful. The committee decided instead that each member would offer their convictions in a fifteen-minute address during televised open-door sessions, after which members would further deliberate. Only then would a recommendation be given to the House. Ironically, Jordan was a reluctant participant. She would have preferred to scrap the speeches, as they would certainly represent passionate partisan interest instead of unbiased reasoned fact-finding.

On July 24 and 25, the House Judiciary Committee convened and its thirty-eight members, twenty-seven Democrats and eleven Republicans, delivered their respective addresses. Among the committee members were future Senate Majority Leader Trent Lott, a Republican from Mississippi where Nixon had won 78 percent of the popular vote, and Congressional Black Caucus cofounder Charles Rangel, a Democrat from New York. The lone other woman on the committee was Elizabeth Holtzman of New York who at age thirty-one was the youngest woman ever to serve in the U.S. House of Representatives.

Jordan was one of the last members of the committee to speak. Notwithstanding her meticulous research and preparation on the issue, she was not entirely sure about what to say. A mere two hours before her scheduled address, she had jotted down four pages of notes taken from her readings on impeachment. She arrived at her Judiciary seat armed with those notes and a chart comparing questionable actions committed by Nixon and various statements on impeachable actions. Her delivery was thus extemporaneous, neither memorized nor written verbatim. At 8:15 P.M. (EST), Judiciary Committee Chair Peter Rodino, a Democrat from New Jersey, turned the floor over to Jordan for her allotted fifteen minutes. The address turned Andy Warhol's notion that everyone gets "fifteen minutes of fame" on its head. Jordan was not "everyone," and those fifteen minutes became a launching point that would help secure Jordan's oratorical place in America's hall of fame.

Before you listen to Jordan's address, and, particularly if you have never heard her before, I offer a couple of pieces of listening advice. First, remove all unnecessary distractions from your listening environment. Second, play the speech through stereo speakers and turn the volume up to a level where you can comfortably hear the full dynamic range of her voice. Finally, remember that the voice you will hear comes from a southern black woman from Houston, Texas, so be prepared for some discernible evidence of that in her verbal delivery.

"Today I Am an Inquisitor"

Mr. Chairman, I join my colleague Mr. Rangel in thanking you for giving the junior members of this committee the glorious opportunity of sharing the pain of this inquiry. Mr. Chairman, you are a strong man, and it has not been easy but we have tried as best we can to give you as much assistance as possible.

Pause the audio! If this is your first taste of Jordan's verbal delivery, chances are good that you are a bit surprised, perhaps even confused, as to how to relate the voice you are hearing to Jordan's identity as a southern, black woman only recently come to Washington, D.C., as a tried-and-true-blue Texas democrat. You are not alone. Jordan's verbal delivery will surprise native Houstonians as much as it does the rest of us. Missing, for instance, is any trace of that stereotypical Texas accent. The long vowel "a" in "Rangel" is not pronounced as an "i" like "pie"; the long vowel "i" in "tried" is not pronounced "ah" as in "trod." Indeed, there does not seem to be anything specifically "Texan" or generally "southern" about her accent at all.

We might have expected Jordan to adopt at least a few of those verbal qualities that would have put her in good stead with the good old boys of her state's party politics. She could have emulated the West Texas drawl of former president Lyndon Baines Johnson, perhaps the most prominent member of the old boys' club at the time. Johnson, whom Jordan admired and sought advice from, had already influenced her selection for the Judiciary Committee. Perhaps it was because Johnson's drawl, however appropriate in some political circles, was the target of criticism and even mockery among members of his own party outside the South.

There was also Jordan's friend and rising politician Ann Richards, who would later become governor of Texas and whose 1988 Democratic National Convention keynote address, in thickly and unabashedly southern twang, turned more than a few heads with the insinuation that George H. W. Bush was less than credible because he lacked an authentic Texas accent. But no trace of Richards's distinctly Texas style can be found in Jordan's speech.

Of course, accent is just one of many verbal properties by which to compare and contrast Jordan's unique verbal delivery. Looking to other notable politicians from her state, particularly those who share Jordan's gender, hardly helps to understand her delivery. The deep resonance of Jordan's voice starkly contrasts with the airy, higher-pitched vocalities of Texas political luminaries Sarah Weddington, who represented "Jane Roe" in the landmark U.S. Supreme Court case *Roe v. Wade*, and current U.S. Senator Kay Bailey Hutchinson. Jordan's voice certainly moves against stereotyped expectations of the "typical southern black woman."

What we do hear is an introductory statement delivered in relatively low-pitched, subdued, but quietly intense tones. Not to be missed is the very smooth delivery of twenty-two words in succession, beginning with "in thanking" and ending with "this inquiry," without a single stutter and punctuated with one of the longer pauses of the entire speech. A full 1.4 seconds pass before Jordan picks up her delivery. In the language of the theater, this is a remarkably articulate opening line followed by an equally articulate dramatic pause. By the power of delivery alone, Jordan has seized her audience's attention.

> *Earlier today, we heard the beginning of the Preamble to the Constitution of the United States: "We, the people." It's a very eloquent beginning. But when that document was completed on the seventeenth of September in 1787, I was not included in that "We, the people." I felt somehow for many years that George Washington and Alexander Hamilton just left me out by mistake. But through the process of amendment, interpretation, and court decision, I have finally been included in "We, the people."*

Raising her volume and vocal pitch, Jordan's voice assumes a qualitatively distinct tone of authority that will mark her verbal delivery for the remainder of the speech. Among the two dozen other speeches delivered by members of the House Judiciary Committee, no other single voice even begins to stand out in terms of sheer authoritative tone.

An interesting content moment occurs in Jordan's allusion to the formerly narrow interpretation of the Constitution, which, in excluding blacks from "the people," gave the included "people" de facto rights for the provision for slavery. Its subsequent and more broadly based interpretation allows Jordan, an African-American and a woman, to embody the very ideals of the more inclusive interpretation of the Constitution. Two delivery points here mark the way in which this particular content moment is regarded. The statement that finds Jordan feeling "left . . . out by mistake" could easily have been taken as a lighthearted gesture toward a very uncivil period. Slavery, as a legally permissible institution of exploitation, had been abolished for more than a hundred years, and Washington and Hamilton were not alone in their slavery-friendly interpretations of the Constitution's preamble. Jordan's tone remains resolved in its severity, and thus we are enjoined to the remark seriously, however rationally difficult it may be to accept the charge at a literal level.

One other point about Jordan's delivery here. If you listen carefully to the passage above, you will notice a slight but discernible verbal variation between the first two instances of "We, the people" and the last instance. The first two instances are similarly declaratory in tone, stated rather firmly in a matter-of-fact style. In the last instance, the tone is somewhat rueful, with Jordan's pitch and volume descending to a place of closure with which she allows her audience to breathe a collective sigh of relief.

> *Today I am an inquisitor. An hyperbole would not be fictional and would not overstate the solemnness that I feel right now. My faith in the Constitution is whole; it is complete; it is total. And I am not going to sit here and be an idle spectator to the diminution, the subversion, the destruction, of the Constitution.*

This section is exemplary in fitting delivery with content. The anaphoric figure following the first instance of "Constitution" is delivered with precious little pause and the anaphoric figure immediately preceding the second instance of "Constitution" is delivered with similar pacing. Both convey a sense of determined reverence marking the occasion. Jordan's delivery has now hit its stride. Elevated levels of volume and pitch, markedly louder and higher than in the opening moments, will become normative markers for the rest of the address. Indeed, volume and pitch variations will take on rhetorical significance only as they deviate in one direction or the other from the present levels. So, too, does Jordan's authoritative tone settle into a normative level of tempered passion. The remaining analysis will point out only those instances in which something special is done in terms of delivery.

I will leave the majority of the rest of Jordan's address to the company of your ears. You will find her tone, pitch, volume, smoothness, and other aspects of delivery to be consistently effective throughout. You will likely also find some delivery moments that seem particularly striking to you. I note for the record that Jordan stutters only twice through the entire speech, an entirely remarkable feat given the content of her address and also given her extemporaneous delivery. We have already seen how easy it is for some speakers, even with the aid of a teleprompter—or even two or more teleprompters containing every single word to be delivered right in front of them—to find delivery an enormous challenge, those who should be representing not only our best interests but our best hopes for brighter rhetorical future. Let us hope that future election years provide exemplary models of oratorical excellence as befits the best in all of us.

That brings us to the final moment in this analysis.

If the impeachment provision in the Constitution
of the United States will not reach the offenses
charged here, then perhaps that eighteenth-century
Constitution should be abandoned to a twentieth-
century paper shredder.

This was the penultimate moment of the address and it struck with atomic rhetorical force that continues to reverberate in the hall and chambers of Congress long after its initial moment of delivery. That force was fashioned through a well-struck balance between content and delivery. In terms of content, the rational power of Jordan's speech up to this point gained force primarily by citing and interpreting various constitutional authorities. That is, it was largely an interpretive venture, with Jordan, the educator, lecturing on the nature of presidential impeachment and the principles and processes regulating constitutional interpretation. Here, Jordan cashes in the significance of her case and moves from the ethos of an educator to that of a judge.

Content alone is not enough to carry such a transition in ethos, and Jordan's sharp and uncharacteristically abrasive tone finds its proper proportion as Jordan ventures from the expositional to the judgmental. Perhaps ironically, this is the one time that Jordan's delivery seems calculated to move the audience beyond mere reason and into a state of passion. No American, regardless of political conviction, can listen impassively to a statement advocating the shredding of America's most revered political document. And only after a speaker has taken great pains to establish his or her ethos on the matter could that speaker possibly hope to deliver such an incendiary statement with the hopes of securing sober conviction.

In a less capable rhetorical voice, the line might just as well have been taken as a joke, something to soothe the tension wrought by listening to twelve minutes of a rather damning lecture. No one, not Jordan's colleagues, not the members of the White House cabinet or staff, not the members of the U.S. Supreme Court, and most certainly not President Nixon himself could find any place for amused relief. Her delivery simply forecloses any possibility of finding humor in the use of a metaphor stretched to ludicrous proportions. To vary that metaphor, the delivery of this particular line, marking as it does a radical departure from its rational precedent, simply and for all practical rhetorical purposes, levels the White House.

The executive branch had been called out and then brought down by a voice that rang out from the legislative branch. The aftermath was a very real and not just rhetorical leveling among the separate powers of government, as the eventual vote of Congress and the subsequent departure of Nixon attests. To take the metaphor further, Jordan's speech was the tipping point in that leveling process. The dam of corruption had been breached and the tide of public sentiment had spilled over, almost overnight, into the troughs of democratic justice. Perhaps most significantly, Jordan's address accomplished something that none of the branches, including Congress, had been able to do to that point. It convinced the American people that their representatives really could speak truth to power to the masses on their own terms and, at the same time, speak with persuasive authority to those within their own ideological ranks. As the next day's papers would acknowledge universally from coast to coast, it was the "thundering" power of Jordan's "godlike" voice that brought constitutional light into the furthest reaches of executive privilege and thereby preserved the balance of power necessary to the health of our government and our nation.

The Tipping Point

Jordan's address at the Nixon impeachment hearings has stood the test of time. Her constitutional lecture serves as a refresher course for erstwhile politicians and government-appointed attorneys who have since had the opportunity to consider and even pursue presidential impeachment charges, as prosecutor Ken Starr's pursuit of President William Jefferson Clinton suggests. But Ken Starr was no Barbara Jordan, and in the end a favorable ruling by the House on charges of perjury failed to make up for the lack of rhetorical authority requisite to win approval in the Senate.

More recently, Congresswoman Shelia Jackson-Lee, in an obvious gesture to Jordan's heroics, took the paper-shredding metaphor to its performative conclusion by holding up a facsimile of the Constitution and ripping it apart during a House floor speech opposing the Bush administration's proposed changes to the Foreign Intelligence Surveillance Act (FISA). The contrived and calculated theatrics probably did not rank among her best congressional moments. But they did bear testimony to the enduring legacy of one of the most remarkable rhetorical episodes in national political history, where one citizen's powers of delivery created a singular authority to speak to and about an issue of the most vital consequence for our nation.

7

Special Rhetorical Tactics

Mary Fisher's 1992 Republican National Convention Address

How DO YOU get two wildly different audiences to thoughtfully consider a topic neither one wants to hear about—at the same time? If you're Mary Fisher, addressing moderate and conservative Republications on the then taboo topic of HIV/AIDS, you adopt a variety of rhetorical tactics. And if you're Mary Fisher at the 1992 Republican National Convention, you do so with great success.

Mary Fisher

Mary Fisher (April 6, 1948–) was born Lizabeth Davis Frehling to George and Marjorie Frehling in Louisville, Kentucky. Marjorie, who did not care for her daughter's given first name, lobbied successfully to get it changed to "Mary," after Mary's great-grandmother, Mary Davis Matz. After four years of marriage, Mary Fisher's parents were divorced, and Marjorie married Max Fisher, a highly successful businessman, philanthropist, and devout Zionist from Detroit, with whom Mary would develop a lifelong and generally endearing relationship.

An influential leader within a number of important Jewish organizations, including the Council of Jewish Federations, the American Jewish Committee, and the United Jewish Appeal, Max Fisher became a confidant and advisor to Israeli prime ministers Golda Meir and Levi Eshkol as well as U.S. presidents Richard M. Nixon and Gerald Ford. As a result, Mary Fisher was introduced to politics at any early age—and at the highest levels. Indeed, her escort at an inaugural dinner for Nixon was a young, lanky Texan named George W. Bush. In addition to his political interests, Max Fisher accumulated a vast fortune through his business dealings so that by the time of his death in 2004, he had achieved an estimated net worth of between 700 and 800 million dollars.

Mary Fisher's privileged upbringing was not without its predictable trappings. Her autobiography, *My Name Is Mary*, from which much of the information in this section is taken, is an often illuminating psychological and spiritual account of her journey. Driven by a need for the assurance of others and perhaps by high parental expectations, the young Mary Fisher fell into people-pleasing patterns of behavior that were as debilitating as they were successful. Popular with teachers and classmates alike, Fisher was voted class president of her high school four years running while at the same time developing a dependency on prescription drugs—to curb her weight, to help her sleep, to calm her nerves—that, in her own words, turned her into "a walking pharmacy" by the time of her high school graduation.

Her successes continued after high school where at the ABC Detroit affiliate WXYZ she moved from secretary to morning show producer in record time. Owing to a combination of her people-managing talents, her organization skills, and her father's reputation, Fisher the producer landed a number of high profile guests for her station's morning program, including the relatively reclusive Henry Ford and later the bombastic Muhammad Ali.

"Mattering" would be an ongoing sentiment in Fisher's personal and professional life. Though hardly exclusive to women of the "New South," a psychological dissonance is perhaps more keenly felt by women there, where the deep desire to live up to a traditional image of the "southern female" often collides with opposing norms requisite to establishing a successful career in "a man's world." It is not easy to navigate between these two extremes, but, as we shall see and hear, Fisher's experiences with these competing standards is in many respects emblematic of the tactically tricky rhetorical course she was forced to chart during her history-making speech at the 1992 Republican National Convention.

After exhausting her interest in local media production, Fisher next used her talents for planning and organizing events for an unanticipated turn into politics. Her father asked her to rescue an event to be put on by the Michigan Republicans at which the recently impeached President Nixon had been originally scheduled to deliver the keynote address and which was now lacking a keynote speaker. Fisher's planning and people-management skills were instrumental in bringing much needed order to the chaos following the Nixon debacle. Along the way, Fisher became, in her words, the "White House's 'key contact' in

Detroit" and, following other strategic planning for various political events on behalf of the Republican Party, she was eventually appointed "presidential advanceman" for Gerald Ford at the ripe age of twenty-seven. The real news, however, had less to do with her age and much more to do with her gender, as the title "presidential advanceman" suspiciously suggests. Mary Fisher became the first woman ever to hold such a position on a U.S. president's advance team. As a result, Fisher had become a D.C. Republican insider by the end of Ford's term in office.

In the ensuing years, Fisher would experience many emotional highs and lows, both personally and professionally. A modestly successful craft and gift company, Mary Fisher Associates, brought her much personal gratification but eventually folded in the wake of litigation arising from charges of design infringement. Her first marriage in 1977 saw the birth of her son, Max, but ended in divorce less than a year later. Fisher's second marriage to artist Brian Campbell, which led to the adoption of a second son, Zachary, also ended in divorce. Her battle with alcoholism and substance abuse landed her in the Betty Ford Clinic.

In late May of 1991, former husband Campbell informed Fisher by phone that he had tested positive for HIV, and Fisher underwent anonymous testing for HIV under the name "Cher." A phone call from the clinic confirmed the worst. Mary Fisher had been infected with HIV, a revelation that brought home for her—and later for many others—that the virus was no respecter of sex, race, political party, or religious ideology. It was this revelation that served as an important catalyst for Mary Fisher's emotional address at the 1992 Republican National Convention in Houston, Texas.

Special Rhetorical Tactics

Beyond the five fundamental categories of public speaking, several rhetorical tactics merit special consideration, not only because they tend to be underappreciated for their tactical significance but also because they are, when identified, genuinely fun to listen to and easy to implement in one's own speeches.

Narratives and Narrative Frames

Everyone likes a good story. Often the most attractive and compelling stories merge celebrity with tragedy, such as the rise of a person to the heights of fame and glory only to meet with a tragic demise. Stories are, by design, selective—they rearrange, re-present, omit, and revise a small number of the available pool of "facts" of a situation, and thereby create a perspective by which to make sense of reality. Thus, any single narrative may offer us a great story, but never the whole story. Moreover, stories bring the past to life in the immediate dynamic of the present, compelling us emotionally to come to terms with that present. At their best, stories engage the rational and imaginative aspects of human cognition and at a very personal level leave us with a sense that "It could happen to me" or alternatively "There but for the grace of God go I."

Narrative frames present a larger portrait for us to consider. They constitute the lenses through which we make sense of a narrative. Sometimes the frame is marked by obvious cues as to how to perceive narrative content. Contemporary television shows such as "The Colbert Report" are framed ironically so that no matter how serious the content a news report appears to be, the ironic frame ensures that no one will take that content at face value. Some social commentators have traced the function of lyrics in hip-hop music to the inner city verbal contests in which young men "diss" each other as a way to bolster the personas of the contestants and to establish a cultural sense of masculinity. A cultural outsider unaware of the "street tough" frame may well wonder how these young men could possibly remain on good terms during and after such insults and even threats of violence. Irony and "street tough" are just two kinds of narrative frames that help us to interpret the content of those narratives. There are political, religious, and other cultural frames that color the way content is created and perceived.

Rhetorically considered, narratives and narrative framing provide compelling pictures that encourage a particular view of reality and therefore discourage alternative views. The persuasive power of narrative is found in how the choice, arrangement, and augmentation of "facts" compel our reason and imagination toward a particular rhetorical end. The persuasive power of narrative frames is found in how a given narrative is to be "seen" in a larger context. Both modes of persuasion played important roles in how audiences viewed Mary Fisher, her story, and themselves in coming to terms with what was then considered an inappropriate and deadly silence on the problem of HIV/AIDS.

The Cultural Maxim

A cultural maxim is a statement that conveys a general or probable truth intrinsic to a given culture or subculture. It is a statement whose expression has become so familiar that it has passed beyond the realm of applied thought and into the realm of unquestioned common sense. Maxims are as ubiquitous as they are familiar. You'll find them in the air, "Birds of a feather flock together." You'll find them near the sea, "Don't go in the water until you learn how to swim." You'll find them in your yard, "Good fences make good neighbors," your house, "Every family has a skeleton in the closet," and even up a tree, "She who plants a tree plants for posterity."

For years leading maximologists have argued that cultural maxims have only one natural enemy: other maxims. The classic textbook example had it that if you try to woo someone under the advice that "Absence makes the heart grow fonder," you're in for a very short courtship indeed if the object of your affections has you "Out of sight, out of mind." Other examples abound. How satisfying can an act of perseverance be if on the one hand "All good things come to those who wait," and on the other "All good things must come to an end"? How happily can we abide truth where "honesty is the best policy" and also where "the devil is in the details"?

Cultural maxims often function to establish common ground between different audiences and between those audiences and the speaker. Jesse Jackson's much heralded 1984 address to the Democratic National Convention contained the following maxim: "I am not a perfect servant. I am a public servant doing my best against the odds. As I develop and serve, be patient: God is not finished with me yet." The maxim "God is not finished with me yet," drawn from a religious subculture, served to explain and ultimately justify some of the controversial statements Jackson had made during the course of his historic 1984 presidential campaign. Audiences reacted immediately and without apparently serious thought with sustained applause. Jackson's maxim had its rhetorical moment of glory. Well deployed, cultural maxims require no further discussion. In this sense, maxims serve to deflect and even shut down specific questions that might be asked of a given rhetorical situation. In Jackson's case, those questions might have revolved around his criticism of eventual Democratic presidential nominee Walter Mondale as a second-rate Hubert Humphrey. And, was Jackson really serving his party's best interests when he referred to the process of selecting a vice presidential candidate as a "public relations parade of personalities"?

More recent investigations into the power of cultural maxims have uncovered another enemy of the cultural maxim: rational inquiry. Namely, maxims can be called into account for oversimplifying otherwise complex problems. In the case of Jesse Jackson, religion may be one among a number of forces necessary to character adjustment, political expediency being among the most obvious. It is not likely that Jackson would have been brought to such a statement had there not been significant political fallout from his criticisms. Legal forces, too, come into play when drawing the line between legitimate name-calling rhetoric frequent in much political campaign rhetoric and outright slander. Thus, cultural maxims, as effective as they can be, do have natural rhetorical enemies in opposing cultural maxims and in the charge of oversimplification.

Master Metaphors

In Chapter 5 I discussed the role that metaphor plays in the process of speechmaking. There, we treated metaphor as a figure of speech that provides a new or different perspective on an old idea via the process of comparison. In this chapter we elevate the status of metaphor both qualitatively and quantitatively. Qualitatively, we will treat the purpose and effect of metaphor not in relation to a single idea or even set of ideas within a given speech but rather as an ultimate grounding perspective by which the content of an entire speech may be interpreted.

At this all-encompassing level, it is as though we are given special lenses through which all content is colored and shaped. One example, related to the speech in this chapter, concerns the use of a metaphor to make sense of how antiretroviral drugs are used against HIV/AIDS. The metaphor "tag team cocktail therapy" refers to the simultaneous use of different drugs whose cumulative effect works by giving the virus different "opponents" to fight at almost the same time. When the virus begins working against one drug, another drug takes over to fight the virus anew. The metaphor helps us to avoid the confusing technical jargon used by medical experts such as "Protease inhibitors," "fusion inhibitors," and "entry inhibitors," and provides a way of understanding an entire range of scientific concepts and applications in easy-to-digest terms, even if these terms are more readily associated with alcohol consumption and wrestling.

The quantitative dimension concerns the degree of persuasive force granted to a metaphor. The statements "Public speaking is a fundamental spoke in the wheel of American democracy" and "Public speaking is a necessary cylinder in the engine that drives American democracy" vary in their degree of rhetorical force. Both capture the relationship of the part (rhetoric) to the whole (democracy). But the second metaphor carries more force, not simply because automobiles are more powerful than bicycles but also because you can ride a bike missing one or more spokes and not lose any capacity for speed. Take out a cylinder and you've lost quite a bit.

Theory of Tactics

Narratives and *narrative frames*, *cultural maxims*, and *master metaphors* are key rhetorical tactics that can well serve a speaker's rhetorical goals. Each tactic shapes human perceptions of reality to strategic ends. Narrative and narrative frames shape perception through a coherent and compelling arrangement of facts, bringing the past to life and making it significant for the present. Cultural maxims offer generally accepted, quick-hitting moral "truths" by which to explain and justify controversial outcomes. Master metaphors provide a final grounding perspective for the overall content of a speech and work with greater persuasive force than less powerful, competing metaphors. As we will see and hear shortly, each of these tactics was used separately to significant effect. But in combination, working together, they would prove to provide devastatingly powerful instruments of persuasion that would help Fisher avoid both apathy and vitriol from audiences who did not want to hear Fisher's message, let alone allow themselves to be moved by it.

Scylla and Charybdis at the Republican National Convention

In Homer's *Odyssey*, Scylla and Charybdis are two sea monsters who dwell on either side of a channel that runs between the eastern tip of Sicily and southern Italy. Scylla possesses twelve feet and six heads, each with three rows of razor sharp teeth. Sail too close to her and you'll be eaten alive. On the other side is Charybdis, who is all mouth. Several times a day she sucks water in and regurgitates it back out with a force violent enough to drown any hapless seafaring vessel foolish enough to sail too close to her wake. The creatures are personifications of two navigational hazards flanking the channel. It is from this story that we get the proverbial "rock and a hard place."

This myth provides the launching point for discussion of the two primary audiences and their respective interests that constituted the rhetorical "dangers" through which Fisher's "Whisper of AIDS" address to the Republican National Convention attempted to navigate. On one side lay Republican moderates generally apathetic to the problem of HIV/AIDS as a matter of public moment. On the other side were conservative evangelicals ready and willing to do battle against any and all "enemies of God." Steer too close to the one and your message dissolves into the murky waters of apathy only to be spit back out and taken asunder again in an endless cycle of indifference that is the bane of most lost causes. Sail too close to the other and your message is apt to be destroyed by the kind of hellfire and brimstone that was the special purview of the prophets of old. And, as we shall see, the 1992 Republican National Convention was not without its share of those kinds of prophets.

Two decisively public events occurring prior to the 1992 Republican National Convention offered more than a little cause for hope that Mary Fisher's message might be received. In November of 1991, basketball great Earvin "Magic" Johnson shocked the world with a press conference announcing that he was HIV positive. And in July of 1992, Elizabeth Glaser delivered a stirring address to the nation at the Democratic National Convention detailing her own struggles with HIV/AIDS. These two events helped to move the issue of HIV/AIDS from the margins into the mainstream of national political conscience so that Republican strategists were now faced with a very important rhetorical dilemma: should HIV/AIDS be the subject of public discussion at the convention and, if so, how should it be discussed?

The answers were hardly clear-cut. Any rhetorical response to the issue of HIV/AIDS may well have had to engage at some level with the convictions of conservative evangelical leaders and their constituencies who typically framed the issue exclusively on severely moral grounds. Moreover, Johnson, a black man, and Glaser, a woman, both Democrats, could hardly be expected to provide the kind of compelling images conducive to favorable action among a conservative Republican mainstream flush with the political confidence that follows from twelve consecutive years of leadership in the White House.

The facts are far from clear, but the evidence suggests that GOP strategists settled on the decision to use two different approaches to HIV/AIDS in an attempt to placate all parties.

It may have been that aforementioned confidence that explains the GOP's willingness to sanction one of the most aggressively-styled opening night addresses of any national political convention in memory. Patrick Buchanan delivered the most famous of these opening night addresses. In what came to be known as his "culture war" speech, Buchanan characterized the just-held Democratic National Convention as the "greatest single exhibition of cross-dressing in

American political history." Buchanan's rhetoric thundered against a predictable array of targets including the "homosexual rights movement," "radical feminism," "environmental extremists," and "the raw sewage of pornography." By the time he was finished, Buchanan had constructed his own formidable Charybdis for the less prophetically disposed speakers yet to take the Republican stage as it bellowed out: "Those who pass this way and heed not my message shall perish."

Mary Fisher remained undaunted. She had a story to tell—her story—and she pursued its vision with due and definitive diligence. Fisher specifically requested the opportunity to speak to the convention on prime time television between 10:00 P.M. and 11:00 P.M. (EST). She was offered a five-minute slot at around 9:00 P.M. on what had been themed the convention's "family night." The family part met with Fisher's approval. The time allotment did not. After threatening not to speak at all, Fisher was given ten minutes—including a brief introductory video—under the condition that the published convention program would indicate that her address would last for five minutes only. In the parlance of that convention, individual remarks lasting more than five minutes constituted an actual "speech," a privilege reserved for the relatively few personalities whose "star status" warranted it. Fisher had, despite her years working on behalf of the party, no such status. Fortunately, her father did.

Having secured the time needed to deliver her speech, Fisher turned her attention to the speech itself. By her account, with the convention less than a week away, Fisher had yet to commit anything to paper. In some desperation, Fisher turned to A. James Heynen, president of the Greystone Group Inc., with whom she had worked on previous speeches. Heyden recognized that in this particular rhetorical situation, the force of the message would be inextricably bound with the ethos of the speaker and, as such, advised Fisher to present herself as an honest and vulnerable human being, which, fortunately, was an ethos she did not have to strain to project. To an audience already conditioned by the power of sermonizing rhetoric, the power of deeply personal storytelling done with humility was the best hope for rhetorical success. Fisher agreed and began rehearsing accordingly.

On the morning of August 14 in Boca Raton, Florida, Heynen presented Fisher with the initial draft of the speech. Fisher was moved to tears. After revising the final two paragraphs and adding a couple of additional sentences, Heyden faxed a copy to Republican National Convention speechwriter Clark Judge in Houston, who praised the speech for its style and content. The only real concern of Judge's was the length of the speech. Heynen told Judge that the speech would take nine minutes to deliver, ten minutes including the introductory video. During initial rehearsals, Fisher had delivered the speech in around twelve minutes. Careful coaching brought it to just under nine minutes. All was set for that evening.

A "Whisper of AIDS"

This section breaks from the earlier patterns of analyses by making the rhetorical tactics themselves the primary points of departure. Instead of letting the structure of the speech dictate the flow, we will examine each tactic in turn and provide content from the speech to show how narra-

tive frame, master metaphor, cultural maxim, and identification worked within the speech.

A Road Less Traveled

On August 20, 1992, Mary Fisher addressed the Republican National Convention in Houston for the purposes of
raising the collective, national conscience toward those who
suffer under the grim reality of AIDS and of persuading
moderate and conservative Republicans that HIV/AIDS
must become the subject of legitimate and serious-minded
discussions. Because convention and television audiences
were largely unaware of Fisher and to help prime them to
be favorably disposed toward her HIV/AIDS message, a
video was created about Fisher that aired nationally as well
as at the convention immediately prior to her address.

The video presentation begins with images of a young
Mary Fisher accompanied by a dispassionate male voice-
over narration: "Mary Fisher was raised amid prominence.
Her father, Max Fisher, has been a Republican leader and
presidential advisor for more than three decades. . . ."
The narrative directs attention toward the economic and
political circumstances of Fisher's upbringing and identifies both under a Republican banner. Fisher's "privilege" is
Republican privilege draped in the regalia of Republican
red (and white and blue). By these narrative ingredients,
Fisher's ethos as a "true Republican" born of good Republican stock is constructed. Notably and strategically absent
from the narrative is any specific mention of Fisher's Jewish roots, which could have given way to an altogether
different set of associations to the word "privilege." The
dispassionate male voice is used to create a kind of buffer

between the sheer brutality of the disease itself and the fact that a prominent Republican insider had contracted it.

The narrative construction establishing Fisher as a privileged Republican provides the dramatic point of departure for the narrative's next turn: "A year ago Mary Fisher, who had herself served a White House post under Gerald Ford, discovered she is HIV positive." The direct and starkly expressed news that Fisher was "HIV positive" receives additional buffering in view of the narrative element that she had served in the White House under Gerald Ford. Audiences tempted to think of Fisher as an "illegitimate Republican" are now faced with several forceful narrative reasons to think otherwise.

Perhaps the most important persuasive work Fisher's narrative achieves is using the private aspects of her life to induce public concern about HIV/AIDS. In a few words, the narrative abruptly shifts from an overt establishment of Fisher's public credentials to a far more intimate ethos: "In public or private, Mary says her most important audience is her two children, Max and Zachary." "Mary Fisher" has now become "Mary," with the audience given narrative license to feel it is on a first-name basis with a well-credentialed Republican insider. The shift between public and private is intensified as the narrative invites the audience to experience Fisher's family life on deeply intimate terms. The video's narrative has become the storied embodiment of Fisher's hope: a public presentation of an ostensibly private affair. In the wake, HIV/AIDS can no longer simply be felt as definitively personal or even primarily political. The rough ground has been broken and hard hearts have been stirred. Through the power of narrative, HIV/AIDS has become a societal burden and, hence, a public concern.

With this narrative groundwork laid, a larger narrative frame begins to emerge. The narrative of Fisher and her sons can now legitimately be placed within the province of that most revered of Republican Party platform planks: family values. Put differently, the narrative frame not only legitimizes the publicizing of HIV/AIDS among Republicans through the person of Fisher, it legitimizes for Republicans a public concern about the disease by allying it with traditional family values. And family values are hardly something Republicans should be ashamed of or caught "whispering" about.

At this juncture, Mary Fisher's own voice replaces that of the male narrator and continues to further the family values narrative frame in deeply emotional tones:

> *Tonight when I tuck each of you into bed, I said to you what you've heard me say every night of your lives. Since the moment you came from my body, Max, and the hour you were placed in my arms, Zachary, I have known that I would one day need to give you up. So each night I rehearse for the day when I must give you over. That is why, as I reach for the day's last kiss and hug, you always hear me say the same four words, "Sleep with the angels."*

It might be helpful to realize that alternative narrative framing options were available. The video presentation could have presented a medical frame by which to view HIV, one whose narrative centered on the disease itself—the various treatments, hospital visits, and difficult changes to basic daily routines brought about by the disease. The issue could have been framed along religious lines, risking the exclusionary tendencies such a frame might engender.

But, the framing of HIV/AIDS rightly occurrs along personal and family lines, and in the process offers the best hope for creating a credible ethos for Fisher to speak personally and credibly to her audiences about HIV/AIDS. Pathos, too, works favorably within this narrative frame in producing the kind of sympathy that only a mother's relationship with her children can evoke, perhaps the only real emotional antidote to the kind of righteous indignation wrought by Buchanan's fire-breathing rhetoric.

The video narrative has additional benefits. It provides a plausible story in whose reality all can participate, producing the rational and emotional conviction that "It could happen to you, too." Fisher could also, as she does, leverage the family values frame to command allegiance to her message:

> *I ask no more of you than I ask of myself or of my children. To the millions of you who are grieving, who are frightened, who have suffered the ravages of AIDS firsthand: Have courage, and you will find support. To the millions who are strong, I issue the plea: Set aside prejudice and politics to make room for compassion and sound policy.*

The short-term rhetorical goal of the narrative frame is to put the speaker in a more positive light so the message can be attended to without the usual ideological and emotional trappings associated with HIV/AIDS.

But the use of narrative framing, for all its benefits, cannot by itself bear the rhetorical burden. For there is a glaring omission from the story that gives rise to a burning question: "How did she contract HIV?" The response to that question would be handled by a second rhetorical tactic, the cultural maxim.

Answering the Call

The answer to the burning question of how Mary Fisher had contracted HIV/AIDS is never directly divulged, either in the video or in Fisher's speech. On the surface, it seems an astonishing omission and one that gains additional traction in light of Elizabeth Glaser's poignant address on AIDS at the earlier Democratic National Convention. Glaser had barely gotten past the first few words before declaring that she was HIV positive due to a blood transfusion received while giving birth to her first child. The explanation offered two sources of positive appraisal. It provided a direct response to the question "how" and it offered no room for its audience to dismiss the content of Glaser's speech on simple "lifestyle" grounds. Glaser was a heterosexual woman who contracted the disease under medically necessary circumstances.

But while Fisher fails to answer directly the question of "how," she does not leave the matter merely to the audience's imaginative discretion. What she does do takes us into our second rhetorical tactic of note: the cultural maxim.

> *I would never have asked to be HIV positive, but I believe that in all things there is a purpose.*

The maxim "in all things there is a purpose" is perhaps more familiarly rendered "There is a reason for everything." As with all cultural maxims, there is an immediate ring of truth and also of decorum that makes the intellectual act of critical inquiry appear rude or at least out of step with common sense. Its appeal is located in the realm of faith, namely the comforting faith that evil outcomes are redeemable through good purposes, even if those purposes are never fully understood or even realized. The maxim would have resonated particularly with Republican evangelicals conditioned by religious faith to believe that "all things work for the good." By this cultural maxim, then, Fisher's response would not be seen as dismissive—though at the level of information-seeking it was—but instead as a culturally acceptable way of understanding her plight. Most important, the maxim deflects that natural suspicion arising from Fisher's HIV contraction and thereby clears the way for her discourse to continue.

As mentioned previously, the power of cultural maxims can be undermined by other competing maxims and by the charge of oversimplification. The good news is that there is no immediately apparent cultural maxim to counter Fisher's offering. The concepts of non-purpose, chaos, and randomness, well known in scientific and mathematical fields of expertise, have yet to produce a gripping rhetorical alternative that resonates with the force of the purpose-driven maxim.

However, Fisher's maxim is open to the rational charge of oversimplification, namely in its assumption that outcomes can be reduced to a single, rationally intelligible purpose and that lurking behind bad outcomes is a positive goal, otherwise known as a "blessing in disguise." First, there may be many purposes behind HIV/AIDS—biological, political, individual and collective, intentional or unintentional. It might well be that Fisher contracted HIV for the primary rhetorical purpose of raising our collective, national conscience toward those who suffer with it, for the political purpose of generating policy reform, and for the medical purpose of increasing research efforts against it. There could be a dozen such purposes so that the more audiences think about it, the more a single purpose becomes less satisfying. And, God forbid evangelical audiences be led to consider a "divine purpose" and conclude that HIV/AIDS is a matter of divine vengeance rather than an opportunity to display divine compassion. Fortunately for the audiences, Fisher enlists the service of the last of our rhetorical tactics to be discussed, the master metaphor, and does so at the very beginning of her speech.

Tilling the Ground

> *Less than three months ago at platform hearings in Salt Lake City, I asked the Republican Party to lift the shroud of silence which has been draped over the issue of HIV and AIDS. I have come tonight to bring our silence to an end. I bear a message of challenge, not self-congratulation. I want your attention, not your applause.*

At those platform hearings, Fisher employed the same metaphor, characterizing the problem of HIV/AIDS as darkened by the "shroud of silence." In this speech, the shroud becomes her master metaphor, the primary way of "seeing" the problem of HIV/AIDS. Closer examination will reveal the metaphor working on several levels.

In its most obvious sense, a shroud is a piece of cloth used to cover the body of someone who has died. In some religious contexts a shroud is used to cover the face of the dead person. At this level, the metaphor invites audiences to begin the process of demystifying the specter of HIV/ AIDS. Notice that the metaphor neither asks nor requires us to like what we see. It merely beckons audiences to be willing to view the problem for what it is and thereby take the first step toward legitimizing public discussion about it. The metaphor also suggests that the shroud is illegitimate, that it is an illegitimate covering of something that is still very much alive. The shroud metaphor thus encourages two perspectives, both of which provide a conceptual basis for legitimate public discussion.

In borrowing from a religious context, Fisher's metaphor works at a third level by framing HIV/AIDS as an essentially moral rather than a political, social, or even medical crisis. Perhaps most poignantly, the metaphor plays directly to Fisher's conservative audiences' tendency to see HIV/AIDS in severely (and strict) moral terms and meets them at that level of public debate. The moral perspective given the metaphor is expressed in various places throughout the speech, and clarified specifically in the following passage:

> *In the context of an election year, I ask you, here*
> *in this great hall, or listening in the quiet of your*
> *home, to recognize that AIDS virus is not a political*
> *creature. It does not care whether you are Democrat or*
> *Republican; it does not ask whether you are black or*
> *white, male or female, gay or straight, young or old.*

HIV/AIDS is not a racial issue or a gender issue, or an issue of sexual preference, or an issue of biological age. Shorn of these trappings, HIV/AIDS is fundamentally a moral issue. Near the end of the speech, Fisher brings the full force of this master metaphor to bear:

I ask no more of you than I ask of myself or of my children. To the millions of you who are grieving, who are frightened, who have suffered the ravages of AIDS firsthand: Have courage, and you will find support. To the millions who are strong, I issue the plea: Set aside prejudice and politics to make room for compassion and sound policy.

Consistent with the implications of the shroud metaphor, there is a place for grief. Also consistent with the metaphor, the correct response to the problem is compassion, a decidedly moral disposition, requiring the setting aside of (immoral) prejudice and perhaps amoral politics. "Lifting the shroud" becomes a clarion call to choose the moral high ground in the form of compassion rather than judgment, a place where most Republicans could find room for comfortable participation.

There are, however, at least two dangers associated with making sense of the problem of HIV/AIDS in this way. First, the metaphor runs the risk of incurring the wrath of moderate Republicans wary of framing the debate in conservative-religious terms. To this danger, the metaphor does not slouch toward a dogmatic morality, and certainly not the kind of inflammatory moral rhetoric of earlier convention speakers. The metaphor is cast in the most general kind of compassion in the willingness to help victims cope with the devastating loneliness and alienation that often accompanies HIV/AIDS.

The second risk is that conservative Republican audiences may find that the metaphor does not go far enough into the realm of morality in that it fails to address the moral causes and implications of HIV/AIDS. Against such powerfully held convictions, the shroud metaphor offers

the only thing it really can: gentleness. Unlike temple cur-
tains, shrouds are not ripped apart but rather are gently
removed so as not to do damage to that which is covered.
Moreover, the compassion engendered by the metaphor is
in keeping with much of the ideological thrust of the Bible's
New Testament, a touchstone that conservative evangelicals would naturally use to help make sense of Fisher's
metaphor. Without actually saying it, the shroud metaphor
offers a gentle corrective to an Old Testament morality
whose predominant concern with the law, righteousness,
and judgment is given life-renewing grace through the
New Testament's messages of faith, hope, and love. In these
ways, then, the master metaphor of the "shroud of silence"
attempts to and succeeds in charting a course between the
Charybdis of moderate Republican apathy and the Scylla
of conservative Republican indignation.

A Woman Tested

The 1992 Republican National Convention was a tale of
two markedly divergent rhetorical approaches to winning
the allegiance of the same audience. The "us good guys–
them bad guys" rhetoric of Buchanan has a rich history
in American political discourse, branding in no uncertain
partisan lines its friends and foes with stamps of approval
and disapproval among ears willing to listen. Alongside this
tradition—and as a check and balance against it—Fisher's
speech rings forth like one crying out in the wilderness,
declaiming mercy over judgment and social obligation over
mere individual right. In taming the beasts of moderate
Republican ambivalence and conservative Republican ire,
Fisher has reclaimed anew that most American of Ameri-

can truths: liberty and justice for some is no liberty and justice at all.

In our current political milieu, the rhetorical power of narratives, maxims, and metaphors continues to offer available and compelling means of persuasion. Moreover, as Fisher's oratorical efforts suggest, such tactics are best utilized when woven into a message that a speaker does not merely convey but legitimately embodies: the speaker becomes the message, the message becomes the speaker. And with that lesson, we discover that the great Roman rhetorician Quintilian was only half right. For whether one sees in Fisher's embodied message the outline of the scarlet letter or an archetype of Scarlett O'Hara—both offer redemptive hope in the wake of tragic circumstances—we are left with the quintessential ideal of speechmaking: great oratory is accomplished by the "good [wo]man speaking well."

8

Great Speechmaking

IN THE INTRODUCTION of this book, we considered three questions: What is great oratory? How do we recognize it? What can we thoughtfully say about it? These are the "big" questions that animate the content of this book.

Let's take the first two questions first. Great speechmaking strategically navigates a mix of situation, content, structure, style, and delivery elements to achieve specific persuasive effects with particular audiences—and does so successfully. There is much to consider in that answer, so let's review great oratory's basic categories and ingredients.

Ronald Reagan's Situation

By "situation" we mean a rhetorical context in which a discernible rhetorical problem is or has become so significant to enough people that an immediate response from a speaker to an audience via a public speech becomes a necessary and fitting response. In January of 1986, the dramatic disintegration of the space shuttle *Challenger* on live television left a confused and disheartened American public. Ronald Reagan's *Challenger* address worked strategically to meet disparate affected interest groups on their own terms. To the family and friends of the deceased, Reagan was an empathetic father consoling the bereaved. To NASA employees, he was the ideological champion of the larger principles—the quest for scientific knowledge and the advancement of new technologies—for which the space program was created. For the schoolchildren who witnessed the explosion firsthand, he was the gentle but firm parental figure, reminding them (and us) that great endeavors require great sacrifice, sometimes the ultimate sacrifice. For all of us, Reagan was both our national eulogist through whom we could come to public terms with our private grief and our nation's "leading man" playing out the gritty integrity and unabashed pride that is our national ideological birthright. Great oratory responds fittingly to the demands of the situation.

Edward Kennedy's Content

Content encompasses both the ideas and arguments of a speech as well as the basic appeals used to accomplish a speaker's persuasive purposes. It is common knowledge among professional speechwriters that establishing rapport between speaker and audience is generally a good thing to do and particularly so when that audience is relatively poorly dispositioned against the speaker's ideas, if not the speaker himself. In his address to conservative evangelicals, Edward Kennedy established audience rapport through humor, telling jokes against himself, his family, and even his own political party. These were ethos-building tactics designed to carve out a place where the now appropriately humbled speaker could legitimately make a rational case for his position. This was not to be a contest of icons— Kennedy versus Falwell—but a contest of ideas. Only after Kennedy had taken the edge off the situation and forged a measure of goodwill would he then begin the process of rationally considering the issues at stake. Great speech-making successfully uses content in ways that appeal to both the mind (logos) and the heart (pathos) and is best taken when the source of that content is perceived as trust-worthy, knowledgeable, fair-minded, and sincere.

Douglas MacArthur's Structure

Matter without form is meaningless. Without structure the best laid plans for the content of a speech can never hope to materialize in any sensible way. This does not mean that the content of a speech must follow a strict, generic pattern of organization. It is to say that there must be some kind of organizational pattern, and one calculated to maximize the effect of the message of a speech. Most speeches do orga-nize content in more or less configured sections of intro-duction, body, and conclusion, but from there any number of variations is possible.

Douglas MacArthur's final address at West Point is a model of both microstructure and macrostructure. The motif of his speech was provided by the motto of his beloved West Point institution: "Duty, Honor, Country." MacArthur took the sequence in which the words appear as a cue for the structure of his content. After a few opening lines of rapport, MacArthur moved quickly into the body of his speech, which was arranged topically—as opposed to chronologically or spatially. Here, MacArthur took up in turn the significance of the award meaning and provided a series of poignant images to enlarge and enhance the respective meanings of duty, honor, and country. Within this framework, there was a nuanced emotional structure in which each key term was not only assigned a particular kind of emotional weight but a weight that can only be understood in view of the emotional weight of each other term. In this way, MacArthur, when structuring his speech, made each term dependent upon the other for meaning and significance and thereby brought magnanimous uniformity to the code—Duty, Honor, Country. Finally, in the conclusion, MacArthur began to suggest that the code itself could only be transcended in death. This was only a temporary structural detour, as MacArthur's conclusion came to rest in the final conviction that one's death is only as meaningful as one's life, and for the soldier the meaning and measure of one's life is inextricably bound up with the code. Thus, not even the power of death can transcend the power of the code. In this way, we saw how the meaning of the content of a speech can be enhanced by the way in which it is structured and thus, again, we return to the idea that content without structure is meaningless.

John F. Kennedy's Style

John F. Kennedy's inaugural address has been heralded as one of the greatest political speeches delivered on American soil, not only because of the personal charisma of its deliverer, the substance and arrangement of its main ideas, or even how skillfully it negotiated the parameters of the rhetorical situation. The greatness of Kennedy's address cannot be understood apart from the style through which its substance was conveyed. As with choosing the proper attire for a given social occasion, a speaker dismisses considerations of speech style at great peril to his or her persuasive purposes.

The most poignant moments in a memorable inaugural were oratorical fashion statements as much as they were convictions about Kennedy's agenda. Kennedy's foreign policy was not going to be ruled merely by the potential and actual terrors of the nuclear age. His policy would seek to preserve America's military and industrial strength while holding out the higher and more enduring hope of peace through diplomacy. In other words, Kennedy would have us "never negotiate out of fear, but never fear to negotiate." Likewise, Kennedy implied that American technology would continue to pave the way for a better quality of life but not if that quality was merely a subtext for the downward spiral into nihilism. Kennedy's inaugural address had to be both "high tech" and "high touch" for his vision to be realized. That vision was carefully styled by using the ever-eloquent figure antimetabole: "Ask not what your country can do for you; ask what you can do for your country." Its impact is as immediate now as it was then; indeed, it is one form of style that will probably never go out of fashion.

Kennedy's inaugural is redolent with such fashion(ed) statements, a point which becomes even more apparent if one takes the time to look at the speech on a line-by-line basis. Nearly every single line is laden with ideological substance and invariably buoyed with a form-fitting figure of expression. In the end, Kennedy's address achieved a kind of gravity-defying oratorical feat in which the weight of ideas was met by the force of style, and in that space, a new generation was launched into a new era.

Barbara Jordan's Delivery

Speaking of oratorical force, not many speakers can claim the superlative-engendering reactions offered in descriptive praise of Barbara Jordan's verbal delivery. Indeed with such presiding characterizations as "the voice of God" and "god-like thunder" in reference to the effect that Jordan's delivery had on those fortunate enough to hear it, hers would seem a singularly compelling disproof of Shakespeare's well-trodden dictum about "sound and fury, signifying nothing." To be sure, Shakespeare was no idiot. He was also, even by the heightened standards of verbal delivery given his day, no Barbara Jordan.

It is not easy to give a scientific account of just how Jordan accomplished her spell. We spoke, as we should have, of relevant verbal elements of pitch, rate, tone, pace, volume, inflection, accent, and smoothness combined with the indefinite varieties of manipulation and variation among them, but without any scientifically tested, let alone agreed upon, means of assessing how best the elements should work together. Perhaps this is as it should be. Verbal delivery is, in the final analysis, more a matter of artistic negotiation than scientific manipulation. In this, and dictums on delivery notwithstanding, great oratory probably has more in common with Shakespeare than with Einstein.

Mary Fisher's Special Tactics

Caught between a rock and a hard place of Homeric proportions, Mary Fisher sought to champion the cause of the millions of victims of HIV and AIDS by delivering an address to the Republican National Convention that had to steer a course between conservative Republican antipathy and moderate Republican indifference.

In service of this cause, Fisher was not alone. Before she uttered a word, a potent video narrative set the tenor and tone for the speech that would follow. In that narrative, Fisher was portrayed as a credible Republican American figure on one side and also as a sympathetic figure emblematic of the silent suffering on the part of those similarly afflicted. More important, the narrative presented a plausible reality—divorced from the ideological trappings of sexual preference and political persuasion—that everyone in her audience, both conservative and moderate Republican alike, could find legitimate. That is, a story that cried out, "If it happened to me, it could happen to you." By this narrative, HIV/AIDS was positioned to become the subject of legitimate public discussion among those who theretofore had little incentive to treat it either publicly or legitimately.

As Fisher began and moved into her speech, two key tactics emerged to help bolster the opening narrative's effects. First, although the narrative indicated that Fisher had contracted HIV, no information was given as to how she did. The question would be of vital importance for socially conservative Republicans who would have been more easily able to dismiss Fisher in the same way that Patrick Buchanan had dismissed any notions of humility toward and empathy with those people whose chosen lifestyle were deemed hazardous to traditional American culture.

Fisher's response came in the form of a cultural maxim: "I believe that in all things there is a purpose." Cultural maxims carry the force of "self-evident truth" and combine with it the force of social propriety. Working in tandem, the two forces make the intellectual act of critical inquiry appear rude or at least out of step with common decency. The net effect is to transform the question of "how" into the broader question of "why," so that the discussion now becomes centered squarely on the larger meaning of and implications of AIDS upon society. That discussion was explicitly drawn into spiritual/religious quarters by Fisher's "shroud of silence" metaphor. As noted, the associations granted a "shroud"—as a symbol of legitimate public grieving and as an inappropriate covering for something that is very much alive (people with HIV/AIDS) and hence something to be "lifted"—became a powerful alternative frame through which to consider the question of HIV/AIDS as a public problem among and between conservative and moderate Republicans.

So, perhaps now you have a better understanding of the attributes of great oratory. At one level we recognize great oratory in terms of general categories—situation, content, structure, style, and delivery. At another level, we can observe the concrete manifestations of those categories in some of the finest public speeches delivered on American soil in the twentieth century.

There is a final issue to consider. What if someone asks you the question, What is great oratory? How might you thoughtfully respond? I might suggest at the outset that overly and overtly intellectualized responses tend to succeed only in shifting the target of the question from the subject of oratory to the subject of the person talking about it. What I find fruitful is to first rattle off some lines from a great speech and then discuss those lines in terms of, say, style. Most have heard of JFK's "Ask not . . ." line but few would know the name of the figure of speech. If you could recite several different lines and then name the figures you could then suggest that these figures are part of the *style* of great oratory. And from there you could well attract some discussion on how and why the category of style contributes to great speechmaking. And of course, there are four additional categories waiting in the wings.

Larger questions about oratory remain. While Aristotle's analytic view of oratory has dominated the analysis of speeches in this book, Plato's concerns remain. Who is to say where the line is to be drawn in Edward Kennedy's address between flattering an audience for self-serving purposes and winning their minds and hearts in service to the collective good? Arguments that treat oratory as merely an acquired habit of or experience with rousing the desires and emotions of an audience to gain one's way with them will find more than a little evidence across a number of oratorical moments in this book to support such a Platonic view. Perhaps it is safest to say that the Great Debate is hardly settled and that different contexts, speakers, and situations may tilt the balance in one direction or the other. That is for you, the reader and listener, to decide. Take your time and decide well. The fate of America, of the oratorical expression of American ideals and values, her past, present, and future, her life and death, hang in the balance of your judgment.

Appendix

Speech Transcripts in Their Entirety

Ronald Reagan's Space Shuttle
Challenger Address

January 28, 1986
White House, Washington, DC

Ladies and Gentlemen, I'd planned to speak to you tonight to report on the state of the Union, but the events of earlier today have led me to change those plans. Today is a day for mourning and remembering. Nancy and I are pained to the core by the tragedy of the shuttle *Challenger*. We know we share this pain with all of the people of our country. This is truly a national loss.

Nineteen years ago, almost to the day, we lost three astronauts in a terrible accident on the ground. But we've never lost an astronaut in flight. We've never had a tragedy like this. And perhaps we've forgotten the courage it took for the crew of the shuttle. But they, the *Challenger* Seven, were aware of the dangers, but overcame them and did their jobs brilliantly. We mourn seven heroes: Michael Smith, Dick Scobee, Judith Resnik, Ronald McNair, Ellison Onizuka, Gregory Jarvis, and Christa McAuliffe. We mourn their loss as a nation together.

For the families of the seven, we cannot bear, as you do, the full impact of this tragedy. But we feel the loss, and we're thinking about you so very much. Your loved ones were daring and brave, and they had that special grace, that special spirit that says, "Give me a challenge, and I'll meet it with joy." They had a hunger to explore the universe and discover its truths. They wished to serve, and they did. They served all of us.

We've grown used to wonders in this century. It's hard to dazzle us. But for twenty-five years the United States space program has been doing just that. We've grown used to the idea of space, and, perhaps we forget that we've only just begun. We're still pioneers. They, the members of the *Challenger* crew, were pioneers.

And I want to say something to the schoolchildren of America who were watching the live coverage of the shuttle's take-off. I know it's hard to understand, but sometimes painful things like this happen. It's all part of the process of exploration and discovery. It's all part of taking a chance and expanding man's horizons. The future doesn't belong to the fainthearted; it belongs to the brave. The *Challenger* crew was pulling us into the future, and we'll continue to follow them.

I've always had great faith in and respect for our space program. And what happened today does nothing to diminish it. We don't hide our space program. We don't keep secrets and cover things up. We do it all up front and in public. That's the way freedom is, and we wouldn't change it for a minute.

We'll continue our quest in space. There will be more shuttle flights and more shuttle crews and, yes, more volunteers, more civilians, more teachers in space. Nothing ends here; our hopes and our journeys continue.

I want to add that I wish I could talk to every man and woman who works for NASA, or who worked on this mission and tell them: "Your dedication and professionalism have moved and impressed us for decades. And we know of your anguish. We share it."

There's a coincidence today. On this day three hundred and ninety years ago, the great explorer Sir Francis Drake died aboard ship off the coast of Panama. In his lifetime the great frontiers were the oceans, and a historian later said, "He lived by the sea, died on it, and was buried in it." Well, today, we can say of the *Challenger* crew: Their dedication was, like Drake's, complete.

The crew of the space shuttle *Challenger* honored us by the manner in which they lived their lives. We will never forget them, nor the last time we saw them, this morning, as they prepared for their journey and waved goodbye and "slipped the surly bonds of earth" to "touch the face of God."

Thank you.

Edward M. Kennedy's "Faith and Country, Tolerance and Truth in America"

October 3, 1983
Liberty Baptist College (Now Liberty University), Lynchburg, Virginia

Thank you very much Professor Kombay for that generous introduction. And let me say, that I never expected to hear such kind words from Dr. Falwell. So in return, I have an invitation of my own. On January 20th, 1985, I hope Dr. Falwell will say a prayer at the inauguration of the next Democratic President of the United States. Now, Dr. Falwell, I'm not exactly sure how you feel about that. You might not appreciate the President, but the Democrats certainly would appreciate the prayer.

Actually, a number of people in Washington were surprised that I was invited to speak here—and even more surprised when I accepted the invitation. They seem to think that it's easier for a camel to pass through the eye of the needle than for a Kennedy to come to the campus of Liberty Baptist College. In honor of our meeting, I have asked Dr. Falwell, as your Chancellor, to permit all the students an extra hour next Saturday night before curfew. And in return, I have promised to watch the "Old Time Gospel Hour" next Sunday morning.

I realize that my visit may be a little controversial. But as many of you have heard, Dr. Falwell recently sent me a membership in the Moral Majority—and I didn't even apply for it. And I wonder if that means that I'm a member in good standing.

[Falwell: "Somewhat."]

Somewhat, he says.

This is, of course, a nonpolitical speech which is probably best under the circumstances. Since I am not a candidate for President, it would certainly be inappropriate to ask for your support in this election and probably inaccurate to thank you for it in the last one.

I have come here to discuss my beliefs about faith and country, tolerance and truth in America. I know we begin with certain disagreements; I strongly suspect that at the end of the evening some of our disagreements will remain. But I also hope that tonight and in the months and years ahead, we will always respect the right of others to differ, that we will never lose sight of our own fallibility, that we will view ourselves with a sense of perspective and a sense of humor. After all, in the New Testament, even the Disciples had to be taught to look first to the beam in their own eyes, and only then to the mote in their neighbor's eyes.

I am mindful of that counsel. I am an American and a Catholic; I love my country and treasure my faith. But I do not assume that my conception of patriotism or policy is invariably correct, or that my convictions about religion should command any greater respect than any other faith in this pluralistic society. I believe there surely is such a thing as truth, but who among us can claim a monopoly on it?

There are those who do, and their own words testify to their intolerance. For example, because the Moral Majority has worked with members of different denominations, one fundamentalist group has denounced Dr. Falwell for hastening the ecumenical church and for "yoking together with Roman Catholics, Mormons, and others." I am relieved that Dr. Falwell does not regard that as a sin, and on this issue, he himself has become the target of narrow prejudice. When people agree on public policy, they ought to be able to work together, even while they worship in diverse ways. For truly we are all yoked together as Americans, and the yoke is the happy one of individual freedom and mutual respect.

But in saying that, we cannot and should not turn aside from a deeper and more pressing question—which is whether and how religion should influence government. A generation ago, a presidential candidate had to prove his independence of undue religious influence in public life, and he had to do so partly at the insistence of evangelical Protestants. John Kennedy said at that time: "I believe in an America where there is no religious bloc voting of any kind." Only twenty years later, another candidate was appealing to a[n] evangelical meeting as a religious bloc. Ronald Reagan said to fifteen thousand evangelicals at the Roundtable in Dallas: "I know that you can't endorse me. I want you to know I endorse you and what you are doing."

To many Americans, that pledge was a sign and a symbol of a dangerous breakdown in the separation of church and state. Yet this principle, as vital as it is, is not a simplistic and rigid command. Separation of church and state cannot mean an absolute separation between moral principles and political power. The challenge today is to recall the origin of the principle, to define its purpose, and refine its application to the politics of the present.

The founders of our nation had long and bitter experience with the state, as both the agent and the adversary of particular religious views. In colonial Maryland, Catholics paid a double land tax, and in Pennsylvania they had to list their names on a public roll—an ominous precursor of the first Nazi laws against the Jews. And Jews in turn faced discrimination in all of the thirteen original Colonies. Massachusetts exiled Roger Williams and his congregation for contending that civil government had no right to enforce the Ten Commandments. Virginia harassed Baptist teachers, and also established a religious test for public service, writing into the law that no "popish followers" could hold any office.

But during the Revolution, Catholics, Jews, and Non-Conformists all rallied to the cause and fought valiantly for the American commonwealth—for John Winthrop's "city upon a hill." Afterwards, when the Constitution was ratified and then amended, the framers gave freedom for all religion, and from any established religion, the very first place in the Bill of Rights.

Indeed the framers themselves professed very different faiths: Washington was an Episcopalian, Jefferson a deist, and Adams a Calvinist. And although he had earlier opposed toleration, John Adams later contributed to the building of Catholic churches, and so did George Washington. Thomas Jefferson said his proudest achievement was not the presidency, or the writing of the Declaration of Independence, but drafting the Virginia Statute of Religious Freedom. He stated the vision of the first Americans and the First Amendment very clearly: "The God who gave us life gave us liberty at the same time."

The separation of church and state can sometimes be frustrating for women and men of religious faith. They may be tempted to misuse government in order to impose a value which they cannot persuade others to accept. But once we succumb to that temptation, we step onto a slippery slope where everyone's freedom is at risk. Those who favor censorship should recall that one of the first books ever burned was the first English translation of the Bible. As President Eisenhower warned in 1953, "Don't join the book burners . . . the right to say ideas, the right to record them, and the right to have them accessible to others is unquestioned—or this isn't America." And if that right is denied, at some future day the torch can be turned against any other book or any other belief. Let us never forget: Today's Moral Majority could become tomorrow's persecuted minority.

The danger is as great now as when the founders of the nation first saw it. In 1789, their fear was of factional strife among dozens of denominations. Today there are hundreds—and perhaps even thousands—of faiths and millions of Americans who are outside any fold. Pluralism obviously does not and cannot mean that all of them are right; but it does mean that there are areas where government cannot and should not decide what it is wrong to believe, to think, to read, and to do. As Professor Larry Tribe, one of the nation's leading constitutional scholars has written, "Law in a non-theocratic state cannot measure religious truth, nor can the state impose it."

The real transgression occurs when religion wants government to tell citizens how to live uniquely personal parts of their lives. The failure of Prohibition proves the futility of such an attempt when a majority or even a substantial minority happens to disagree. Some questions may be inherently individual ones, or people may be sharply divided about whether they are. In such cases, like Prohibition and abortion, the proper role of religion is to appeal to the conscience of the individual, not the coercive power of the state.

But there are other questions which are inherently public in nature, which we must decide together as a nation, and where religion and religious values can and should speak to our common conscience. The issue of nuclear war is a compelling example. It is a moral issue; it will be decided by government, not by each individual; and to give any effect to the moral values of their creed, people of faith must speak directly about public policy. The Catholic bishops and the Reverend Billy Graham have every right to stand for the nuclear freeze, and Dr. Falwell has every right to stand against it.

There must be standards for the exercise of such leadership, so that the obligations of belief will not be debased into an opportunity for mere political advantage. But to take a stand at all when a question is both properly public and truly moral is to stand in a long and honored tradition. Many of the great evangelists of the 1800s were in the forefront of the abolitionist movement. In our own time, the Reverend William Sloane Coffin challenged the morality of the war in Vietnam. Pope John XXIII renewed the Gospel's call to social justice. And Dr. Martin Luther King, Jr., who was the greatest prophet of this century, awakened our nation and its conscience to the evil of racial segregation.

Their words have blessed our world. And who now wishes they had been silent? Who would bid Pope John Paul [II] to quiet his voice against the oppression in Eastern Europe, the violence in Central America, or the crying needs of the landless, the hungry, and those who are tortured in so many of the dark political prisons of our time?

President Kennedy, who said that "no religious body should seek to impose its will," also urged religious leaders to state their views and give their commitment when the public debate involved ethical issues. In drawing the line between imposed will and essential witness, we keep church and state separate, and at the same time we recognize that the City of God should speak to the civic duties of men and women.

There are four tests which draw that line and define the difference.

First, we must respect the integrity of religion itself.

People of conscience should be careful how they deal in the word of their Lord. In our own history, religion has been falsely invoked to sanction prejudice—even slavery—to condemn labor unions and public spending for the poor. I believe that the prophecy, "The poor you have always with you," is an indictment, not a commandment. And I respectfully suggest that God has taken no position on the Department of Education—and that a balanced budget constitutional amendment is a matter of economic analysis, and not heavenly appeals.

Religious values cannot be excluded from every public issue; but not every public issue involves religious values. And how ironic it is when those very values are denied in the name of religion. For example, we are sometimes told that it is wrong to feed the hungry, but that mission is an explicit mandate given to us in the twenty-fifth chapter of Matthew.

Second, we must respect the independent judgments of conscience.

Those who proclaim moral and religious values can offer counsel, but they should not casually treat a position on a public issue as a test of fealty to faith. Just as I disagree with the Catholic bishops on tuition tax credits—which I oppose—so other Catholics can and do disagree with the hierarchy, on the basis of honest conviction, on the question of the nuclear freeze.

Thus, the controversy about the Moral Majority arises not only from its views, but from its name—which, in the minds of many, seems to imply that only one set of public policies is moral and only one majority can possibly be right. Similarly, people are and should be perplexed when the religious lobbying group Christian Voice publishes a morality index of congressional voting records, which judges the morality of senators by their attitude toward Zimbabwe and Taiwan.

Let me offer another illustration. Dr. Falwell has written—and I quote: "To stand against Israel is to stand against God." Now there is no one in the Senate who has stood more firmly for Israel than I have. Yet, I do not doubt the faith of those on the other side. Their error is not one of religion, but of policy. And I hope to be able to persuade them that they are wrong in terms of both America's interest and the justice of Israel's cause.

Respect for conscience is most in jeopardy, and the harmony of our diverse society is most at risk, when we reestablish, directly or indirectly, a religious test for public office. That relic of the colonial era, which is specifically prohibited in the Constitution, has reappeared in recent years. After the last election, the Reverend James Robison warned President Reagan not to surround himself, as the president before him had, "with the counsel of the ungodly." I utterly reject any such standard for any position anywhere in public service. Two centuries ago, the victims were Catholics and Jews. In the 1980s the victims could be atheists; in some other day or decade, they could be the members of the Thomas Road Baptist Church. Indeed, in 1976 I regarded it as unworthy and un-American when some people said or hinted that Jimmy Carter should not be president because he was a born again Christian. We must never judge the fitness of individuals to govern on the bas[is] of where they worship, whether they follow Christ or Moses, whether they are called "born again" or "ungodly." Where it is right to apply moral values to public life, let all of us avoid the temptation to be self-righteous and absolutely certain of ourselves. And if that temptation ever comes, let us recall Winston Churchill's humbling description of an intolerant and inflexible colleague: "There but for the grace of God goes God."

Third, in applying religious values, we must respect the integrity of public debate.

In that debate, faith is no substitute for facts. Critics may oppose the nuclear freeze for what they regard as moral reasons. They have every right to argue that any negotiation with the Soviets is wrong, or that any accommodation with them sanctions their crimes, or that no agreement can be good enough and therefore all agreements only increase the chance of war. I do not believe that, but it surely does not violate the standard of fair public debate to say it. What does violate that standard, what the opponents of the nuclear freeze have no right to do, is to assume that they are infallible, and so any argument against the freeze will do, whether it is false or true.

The nuclear freeze proposal is not unilateral, but bilateral—with equal restraints on the United States and the Soviet Union. The nuclear freeze does not require that we trust the Russians, but demands full and effective verification. The nuclear freeze does not concede a Soviet lead in nuclear weapons, but recognizes that human beings in each great power already have in their fallible hands the overwhelming capacity to remake into a pile of radioactive rubble the earth which God has made.

There is no morality in the mushroom cloud. The black rain of nuclear ashes will fall alike on the just and the unjust. And then it will be too late to wish that we had done the real work of this atomic age—which is to seek a world that is neither red nor dead.

I am perfectly prepared to debate the nuclear freeze on policy grounds, or moral ones. But we should not be forced to discuss phantom issues or false charges. They only deflect us from the urgent task of deciding how best to prevent a planet divided from becoming a planet destroyed.

And it does not advance the debate to contend that the arms race is more divine punishment than human problem, or that in any event, the final days are near. As Pope John said two decades ago, at the opening of the Second Vatican Council: "We must beware of those who burn with zeal, but are not endowed with much sense . . . we must disagree with the prophets of doom, who are always forecasting disasters, as though the end of the earth was at hand." The message which echoes across the years is very clear: The earth is still here; and if we wish to keep it, a prophecy of doom is no alternative to a policy of arms control.

Fourth, and finally, we must respect the motives of those who exercise their right to disagree.

We sorely test our ability to live together if we readily question each other's integrity. It may be harder to restrain our feelings when moral principles are at stake, for they go to the deepest wellsprings of our being. But the more our feelings diverge, the more deeply felt they are, the greater is our obligation to grant the sincerity and essential decency of our fellow citizens on the other side.

Those who favor E.R.A [Equal Rights Amendment] are not "antifamily" or "blasphemers." And their purpose is not "an attack on the Bible." Rather, we believe this is the best way to fix in our national firmament the ideal that not only all men, but all people are created equal. Indeed, my mother, who strongly favors E.R.A., would be surprised to hear that she is antifamily. For my part, I think of the amendment's opponents as wrong on the issue, but not as lacking in moral character.

I could multiply the instances of name-calling, sometimes on both sides. Dr. Falwell is not a "warmonger." And "liberal clergymen" are not, as the Moral Majority suggested in a recent letter, equivalent to "Soviet sympathizers." The critics of official prayer in public schools are not "Pharisees"; many of them are both civil libertarians and believers, who think that families should pray more at home with their children, and attend church and synagogue more faithfully. And people are not sexist because they stand against abortion, and they are not murderers because they believe in free choice. Nor does it help anyone's cause to shout such epithets, or to try and shout a speaker down—which is what happened last April when Dr. Falwell was hissed and heckled at Harvard. So I am doubly grateful for your courtesy here this evening. That was not Harvard's finest hour, but I am happy to say that the loudest applause from the Harvard audience came in defense of Dr. Falwell's right to speak.

In short, I hope for an America where neither "fundamentalist" nor "humanist" will be a dirty word, but a fair description of the different ways in which people of goodwill look at life and into their own souls.

I hope for an America where no president, no public official, no individual will ever be deemed a greater or lesser American because of religious doubt—or religious belief.

I hope for an America where the power of faith will always burn brightly, but where no modern Inquisition of any kind will ever light the fires of fear, coercion, or angry division.

I hope for an America where we can all contend freely and vigorously, but where we will treasure and guard those standards of civility which alone make this nation safe for both democracy and diversity.

Twenty years ago this fall, in New York City, President Kennedy met for the last time with a Protestant assembly. The atmosphere had been transformed since his earlier address during the 1960 campaign to the Houston Ministerial Association. He had spoken there to allay suspicions about his Catholicism, and to answer those who claimed that on the day of his baptism, he was somehow disqualified from becoming President. His speech in Houston and then his election drove that prejudice from the center of our national life. Now, three years later, in November of 1963, he was appearing before the Protestant Council of New York City to reaffirm what he regarded as some fundamental truths. On that occasion, John Kennedy said: "The family of man is not limited to a single race or religion, to a single city, or country . . . the family of man is nearly three billion strong. Most of its members are not white and most of them are not Christian." And as President Kennedy reflected on that reality, he restated an ideal for which he had lived his life—that "the members of this family should be at peace with one another."

That ideal shines across all the generations of our history and all the ages of our faith, carrying with it the most ancient dream. For as the Apostle Paul wrote long ago in Romans: "If it be possible, as much as it lieth in you, live peaceably with all men."

I believe it is possible; the choice lies within us; as fellow citizens, let us live peaceably with each other; as fellow human beings, let us strive to live peaceably with men and women everywhere. Let that be our purpose and our prayer, yours and mine—for ourselves, for our country, and for all the world.

Douglas MacArthur's Thayer Award Acceptance Address

May 12, 1962
United States Military Academy,
West Point, New York

General Westmoreland, General Grove, distinguished guests, and gentlemen of the Corps!

As I was leaving the hotel this morning, a doorman asked me, "Where are you bound for, General?" And when I replied, "West Point," he remarked, "Beautiful place. Have you ever been there before?"

No human being could fail to be deeply moved by such a tribute as this [Thayer Award]. Coming from a profession I have served so long, and a people I have loved so well, it fills me with an emotion I cannot express. But this award is not intended primarily to honor a personality, but to symbolize a great moral code—the code of conduct and chivalry of those who guard this beloved land of culture and ancient descent. That is the animation of this medallion. For all eyes and for all time, it is an expression of the ethics of the American soldier. That I should be integrated in this way with so noble an ideal arouses a sense of pride and yet of humility which will be with me always.

Duty, Honor, Country: Those three hallowed words reverently dictate what you ought to be, what you can be, what you will be. They are your rallying points: to build courage when courage seems to fail; to regain faith when there seems to be little cause for faith; to create hope when hope becomes forlorn.

Unhappily, I possess neither that eloquence of diction, that poetry of imagination, nor that brilliance of metaphor to tell you all that they mean.

The unbelievers will say they are but words, but a slogan, but a flamboyant phrase. Every pedant, every demagogue, every cynic, every hypocrite, every troublemaker, and I am sorry to say, some others of an entirely different character, will try to downgrade them even to the extent of mockery and ridicule.

But these are some of the things they do. They build your basic character. They mold you for your future roles as the custodians of the nation's defense. They make you strong enough to know when you are weak, and brave enough to face yourself when you are afraid. They teach you to be proud and unbending in honest failure, but humble and gentle in success; not to substitute words for actions, not to seek the path of comfort, but to face the stress and spur of difficulty and challenge; to learn to stand up in the storm but to have compassion on those who fall; to master yourself before you seek to master others; to have a heart that is clean, a goal that is high; to learn to laugh, yet never forget how to weep; to reach into the future yet never neglect the past; to be serious yet never to take yourself too seriously; to be modest so that you will remember the simplicity of true greatness, the open mind of true wisdom, the meekness of true strength. They give you a temper of the will, a quality of the imagination, a vigor of the emotions, a freshness of the deep springs of life, a temperamental predominance of courage over timidity, of an appetite for adventure over love of ease. They create in your heart the sense of wonder, the unfailing hope of what next, and the joy and inspiration of life. They teach you in this way to be an officer and a gentleman.

And what sort of soldiers are those you are to lead? Are they reliable? Are they brave? Are they capable of victory? Their story is known to all of you. It is the story of the American man-at-arms. My estimate of him was formed on the battlefield many, many years ago, and has never changed. I regarded him then as I regard him now—as one of the world's noblest figures, not only as one of the finest military characters, but also as one of the most stainless. His name and fame are the birthright of every American citizen. In his youth and strength, his love and loyalty, he gave all that mortality can give.

He needs no eulogy from me or from any other man. He has written his own history and written it in red on his enemy's breast. But when I think of his patience under adversity, of his courage under fire, and of his modesty in victory, I am filled with an emotion of admiration I cannot put into words. He belongs to history as furnishing one of the greatest examples of successful patriotism. He belongs to posterity as the instructor of future generations in the principles of liberty and freedom. He belongs to the present, to us, by his virtues and by his achievements. In twenty campaigns, on a hundred battlefields, around a thousand campfires, I have witnessed that enduring fortitude, that patriotic self-abnegation, and that invincible determination which have carved his statue in the hearts of his people. From one end of the world to the other he has drained deep the chalice of courage.

As I listened to those songs [of the glee club], in memory's eye I could see those staggering columns of the First World War, bending under soggy packs, on many a weary march from dripping dusk to drizzling dawn, slogging ankle-deep through the mire of shell-shocked roads, to form grimly for the attack, blue-lipped, covered with sludge and mud, chilled by the wind and rain, driving home to their objective, and for many, to the judgment seat of God.

I do not know the dignity of their birth, but I do know the glory of their death. They died unquestioning, uncomplaining, with faith in their hearts, and on their lips the hope that we would go on to victory. Always, for them: *Duty, Honor, Country*; always their blood and sweat and tears, as we sought the way and the light and the truth.

And twenty years after, on the other side of the globe, again the filth of murky foxholes, the stench of ghostly trenches, the slime of dripping dugouts; those boiling suns of relentless heat, those torrential rains of devastating storms; the loneliness and utter desolation of jungle trails; the bitterness of long separation from those they loved and cherished; the deadly pestilence of tropical disease; the horror of stricken areas of war; their resolute and determined defense, their swift and sure attack, their indomitable purpose, their complete and decisive victory—always victory. Always through the bloody haze of their last reverberating shot, the vision of gaunt, ghastly men reverently following your password of: *Duty, Honor, Country*.

The code which those words perpetuate embraces the highest moral laws and will stand the test of any ethics or philosophies ever promulgated for the uplift of mankind. Its requirements are for the things that are right, and its restraints are from the things that are wrong.

The soldier, above all other men, is required to practice the greatest act of religious training—sacrifice.

In battle and in the face of danger and death, he discloses those divine attributes which his Maker gave when he created man in his own image. No physical courage and no brute instinct can take the place of the Divine help which alone can sustain him.

However horrible the incidents of war may be, the soldier who is called upon to offer and to give his life for his country is the noblest development of mankind.

You now face a new world—a world of change. The thrust into outer space of the satellite, spheres, and missiles mark the beginning of another epoch in the long story of mankind. In the five or more billions of years the scientists tell us it has taken to form the earth, in the three or more billion years of development of the human race, there has never been a more abrupt or staggering evolution. We deal now not with things of this world alone, but with the illimitable distances and as yet unfathomed mysteries of the universe. We are reaching out for a new and boundless frontier.

We speak in strange terms: of harnessing the cosmic energy; of making winds and tides work for us; of creating unheard synthetic materials to supplement or even replace our old standard basics; to purify sea water for our drink; of mining ocean floors for new fields of wealth and food; of disease preventatives to expand life into the hundreds of years; of controlling the weather for a more equitable distribution of heat and cold, of rain and shine; of space ships to the moon; of the primary target in war, no longer limited to the armed forces of an enemy, but instead to include his civil populations; of ultimate conflict between a united human race and the sinister forces of some other planetary galaxy; of such dreams and fantasies as to make life the most exciting of all time.

And through all this welter of change and development, your mission remains fixed, determined, inviolable: it is to win our wars.

Everything else in your professional career is but corollary to this vital dedication. All other public purposes, all other public projects, all other public needs, great or small, will find others for their accomplishment. But you are the ones who are trained to fight. Yours is the profession of arms, the will to win, the sure knowledge that in war there is no substitute for victory; that if you lose, the nation will be destroyed; that the very obsession of your public service must be: *Duty, Honor, Country.*

Others will debate the controversial issues, national and international, which divide men's minds; but serene, calm, aloof, you stand as the Nation's war-guardian, as its life-guard from the raging tides of international conflict, as its gladiator in the arena of battle. For a century and a half you have defended, guarded, and protected its hallowed traditions of liberty and freedom, of right and justice.

Let civilian voices argue the merits or demerits of our processes of government; whether our strength is being sapped by deficit financing, indulged in too long, by federal paternalism grown too mighty, by power groups grown too arrogant, by politics grown too corrupt, by crime grown too rampant, by morals grown too low, by taxes grown too high, by extremists grown too violent; whether our personal liberties are as thorough and complete as they should be. These great national problems are not for your professional participation or military solution. Your guide-post stands out like a tenfold beacon in the night: *Duty, Honor, Country.*

You are the leaven which binds together the entire fabric of our national system of defense. From your ranks come the great captains who hold the nation's destiny in their hands the moment the war tocsin sounds. The Long Gray Line has never failed us. Were you to do so, a million ghosts in olive drab, in brown khaki, in blue and gray, would rise from their white crosses thundering those magic words: *Duty, Honor, Country.*

This does not mean that you are warmongers.

On the contrary, the soldier, above all other people, prays for peace, for he must suffer and bear the deepest wounds and scars of war.

But always in our ears ring the ominous words of Plato, that wisest of all philosophers: "Only the dead have seen the end of war."

The shadows are lengthening for me. The twilight is here. My days of old have vanished, tone and tint. They have gone glimmering through the dreams of things that were. Their memory is one of wondrous beauty, watered by tears, and coaxed and caressed by the smiles of yesterday. I listen vainly, but with thirsty ears, for the witching melody of faint bugles blowing reveille, of far drums beating the long roll. In my dreams I hear again the crash of guns, the rattle of musketry, the strange, mournful mutter of the battlefield.

But in the evening of my memory, always I come back to West Point.

Always there echoes and re-echoes: *Duty, Honor, Country.*

Today marks my final roll call with you, but I want you to know that when I cross the river my last conscious thoughts will be of The Corps, and The Corps, and The Corps.

I bid you farewell.

John F. Kennedy's Inaugural Address

January 20, 1961
White House, Washington, DC

Vice President Johnson, Mr. Speaker, Mr. Chief Justice, President Eisenhower, Vice President Nixon, President Truman, reverend clergy, fellow citizens:

We observe today not a victory of party, but a celebration of freedom—symbolizing an end, as well as a beginning—signifying renewal, as well as change. For I have sworn before you and Almighty God the same solemn oath our forebears prescribed nearly a century and three-quarters ago.

The world is very different now. For man holds in his mortal hands the power to abolish all forms of human poverty and all forms of human life. And yet the same revolutionary beliefs for which our forebears fought are still at issue around the globe—the belief that the rights of man come not from the generosity of the state, but from the hand of God.

We dare not forget today that we are the heirs of that first revolution. Let the word go forth from this time and place, to friend and foe alike, that the torch has been passed to a new generation of Americans—born in this century, tempered by war, disciplined by a hard and bitter peace, proud of our ancient heritage, and unwilling to witness or permit the slow undoing of those human rights to which this nation has always been committed, and to which we are committed today at home and around the world.

Let every nation know, whether it wishes us well or ill, that we shall pay any price, bear any burden, meet any hardship, support any friend, oppose any foe, to assure the survival and the success of liberty.

This much we pledge—and more.

To those old allies whose cultural and spiritual origins we share, we pledge the loyalty of faithful friends. United there is little we cannot do in a host of cooperative ventures. Divided there is little we can do—for we dare not meet a powerful challenge at odds and split asunder.

To those new states whom we welcome to the ranks of the free, we pledge our word that one form of colonial control shall not have passed away merely to be replaced by a far more iron tyranny. We shall not always expect to find them supporting our view. But we shall always hope to find them strongly supporting their own freedom—and to remember that, in the past, those who foolishly sought power by riding the back of the tiger ended up inside.

To those people in the huts and villages of half the globe struggling to break the bonds of mass misery, we pledge our best efforts to help them help themselves, for whatever period is required—not because the Communists may be doing it, not because we seek their votes, but because it is right. If a free society cannot help the many who are poor, it cannot save the few who are rich.

To our sister republics south of our border, we offer a special pledge: to convert our good words into good deeds, in a new alliance for progress, to assist free men and free governments in casting off the chains of poverty. But this peaceful revolution of hope cannot become the prey of hostile powers. Let all our neighbors know that we shall join with them to oppose aggression or subversion anywhere in the Americas. And let every other power know that this hemisphere intends to remain the master of its own house.

To that world assembly of sovereign states, the United Nations, our last best hope in an age where the instruments of war have far outpaced the instruments of peace, we renew our pledge of support—to prevent it from becoming merely a forum for invective, to strengthen its shield of the new and the weak, and to enlarge the area in which its writ may run.

Finally, to those nations who would make themselves our adversary, we offer not a pledge but a request: that both sides begin anew the quest for peace, before the dark powers of destruction unleashed by science engulf all humanity in planned or accidental self-destruction.

We dare not tempt them with weakness. For only when our arms are sufficient beyond doubt can we be certain beyond doubt that they will never be employed.

But neither can two great and powerful groups of nations take comfort from our present course—both sides overburdened by the cost of modern weapons, both rightly alarmed by the steady spread of the deadly atom, yet both racing to alter that uncertain balance of terror that stays the hand of mankind's final war.

So let us begin anew—remembering on both sides that civility is not a sign of weakness, and sincerity is always subject to proof. Let us never negotiate out of fear, but let us never fear to negotiate.

Let both sides explore what problems unite us instead of belaboring those problems which divide us.

Let both sides, for the first time, formulate serious and precise proposals for the inspection and control of arms, and bring the absolute power to destroy other nations under the absolute control of all nations.

Let both sides seek to invoke the wonders of science instead of its terrors. Together let us explore the stars, conquer the deserts, eradicate disease, tap the ocean depths, and encourage the arts and commerce.

Let both sides unite to heed, in all corners of the earth, the command of Isaiah—to "undo the heavy burdens, and [to] let the oppressed go free."[1]

And, if a beachhead of cooperation may push back the jungle of suspicion, let both sides join in creating a new endeavor—not a new balance of power, but a new world of law—where the strong are just, and the weak secure, and the peace preserved.

All this will not be finished in the first one hundred days. Nor will it be finished in the first one thousand days; nor in the life of this Administration; nor even perhaps in our lifetime on this planet. But let us begin.

In your hands, my fellow citizens, more than mine, will rest the final success or failure of our course. Since this country was founded, each generation of Americans has been summoned to give testimony to its national loyalty. The graves of young Americans who answered the call to service surround the globe.

Now the trumpet summons us again—not as a call to bear arms, though arms we need—not as a call to battle, though embattled we are—but a call to bear the burden of a long twilight struggle, year in and year out, "rejoicing in hope; patient in tribulation,"[2] a struggle against the common enemies of man: tyranny, poverty, disease, and war itself.

Can we forge against these enemies a grand and global alliance, North and South, East and West, that can assure

---

1 Isaiah 58:6 (King James Version of the Holy Bible)

2 Romans 12:12 (King James Version of the Holy Bible)

a more fruitful life for all mankind? Will you join in that historic effort?

In the long history of the world, only a few generations have been granted the role of defending freedom in its hour of maximum danger. I do not shrink from this responsibility—I welcome it. I do not believe that any of us would exchange places with any other people or any other generation. The energy, the faith, the devotion which we bring to this endeavor will light our country and all who serve it. And the glow from that fire can truly light the world.

And so, my fellow Americans, ask not what your country can do for you; ask what you can do for your country.

My fellow citizens of the world, ask not what America will do for you, but what together we can do for the freedom of man.

Finally, whether you are citizens of America or citizens of the world, ask of us here the same high standards of strength and sacrifice which we ask of you. With a good conscience our only sure reward, with history the final judge of our deeds, let us go forth to lead the land we love, asking His blessing and His help, but knowing that here on earth God's work must truly be our own.

Barbara Jordan's Statement
on the Articles of Impeachment

July 25, 1974
Washington, DC

Thank you, Mr. Chairman.

Mr. Chairman, I join my colleague Mr. Rangel in thanking you for giving the junior members of this committee the glorious opportunity of sharing the pain of this inquiry. Mr. Chairman, you are a strong man, and it has not been easy but we have tried as best we can to give you as much assistance as possible.

Earlier today, we heard the beginning of the Preamble to the Constitution of the United States: "We, the people." It's a very eloquent beginning. But when that document was completed on the seventeenth of September in 1787, I was not included in that "We, the people." I felt somehow for many years that George Washington and Alexander Hamilton just left me out by mistake. But through the process of amendment, interpretation, and court decision, I have finally been included in "We, the people."

Today I am an inquisitor. An hyperbole would not be fictional and would not overstate the solemnness that I feel right now. My faith in the Constitution is whole; it is complete; it is total. And I am not going to sit here and be an idle spectator to the diminution, the subversion, the destruction, of the Constitution.

"Who can so properly be the inquisitors for the nation as the representatives of the nation themselves?" "The subjects of its jurisdiction are those offenses which proceed from the misconduct of public men." And that's what we're talk-ing about. In other words, [the jurisdiction comes] from the abuse or violation of some public trust.

It is wrong, I suggest, it is a misreading of the Constitu-tion for any member here to assert that for a member to vote for an article of impeachment means that that member must be convinced that the President should be removed from office. The Constitution doesn't say that. The pow-ers relating to impeachment are an essential check in the hands of the body of the legislature against and upon the encroachments of the executive. The division between the two branches of the legislature, the House and the Senate, assigning to the one the right to accuse and to the other the right to judge, the framers of this Constitution were very astute. They did not make the accusers and the judg-ers—and the judges the same person.

We know the nature of impeachment. We've been talking about it awhile now. It is chiefly designed for the President and his high ministers to somehow be called into account. It is designed to "bridle" the executive if he engages in excesses. "It is designed as a method of national inquest into the conduct of public men." The framers con-fided in the Congress the power if need be, to remove the President in order to strike a delicate balance between a President swollen with power and grown tyrannical, and preservation of the independence of the executive.

The nature of impeachment: a narrowly channeled excep-tion to the separation-of-powers maxim. The Federal Con-vention of 1787 said that. It limited impeachment to high crimes and misdemeanors and discounted and opposed the term "maladministration." "It is to be used only for great misdemeanors," so it was said in the North Carolina ratifi-cation convention. And in the Virginia ratification convention: "We do not trust our liberty to a particular branch. We need one branch to check the other."

"No one need be afraid"—the North Carolina ratification convention—"No one need be afraid that officers who commit oppression will pass with immunity." "Prosecutions of impeachments will seldom fail to agitate the passions of the whole community," said Hamilton in the Federalist Papers, number 65. "We divide into parties more or less friendly or inimical to the accused." I do not mean political parties in that sense.

The drawing of political lines goes to the motivation behind impeachment; but impeachment must proceed within the confines of the constitutional term "high crime[s] and misdemeanors." Of the impeachment process, it was Woodrow Wilson who said that "Nothing short of the grossest offenses against the plain law of the land will suffice to give them speed and effectiveness. Indignation so great as to overgrow party interest may secure a conviction; but nothing else can."

Common sense would be revolted if we engaged upon this process for petty reasons. Congress has a lot to do: Appropriations, Tax Reform, Health Insurance, Campaign Finance Reform, Housing, Environmental Protection, Energy Sufficiency, Mass Transportation. Pettiness cannot be allowed to stand in the face of such overwhelming problems. So today we are not being petty. We are trying to be big, because the task we have before us is a big one.

This morning, in a discussion of the evidence, we were told that the evidence which purports to support the allegations of misuse of the CIA by the President is thin. We're told that that evidence is insufficient. What that recital of the evidence this morning did not include is what the President did know on June the 23rd, 1972.

The President did know that it was Republican money, that it was money from the Committee for the Re-election of the President, which was found in the possession of one of the burglars arrested on June the 17th. What the President did know on the 23rd of June was the prior activities of E. Howard Hunt, which included his participation in the break-in of Daniel Ellsberg's psychiatrist, which included Howard Hunt's participation in the Dita Beard ITT affair, which included Howard Hunt's fabrication of cables designed to discredit the Kennedy Administration.

We were further cautioned today that perhaps these proceedings ought to be delayed because certainly there would be new evidence forthcoming from the President of the United States. There has not even been an obfuscated indication that this committee would receive any additional materials from the President. The committee subpoena is outstanding, and if the President wants to supply that material, the committee sits here. The fact is that on yesterday, the American people waited with great anxiety for eight hours, not knowing whether their President would obey an order of the Supreme Court of the United States.

At this point, I would like to juxtapose a few of the impeachment criteria with some of the actions the President has engaged in. Impeachment criteria: James Madison, from the Virginia ratification convention. "If the President be connected in any suspicious manner with any person and there be grounds to believe that he will shelter him, he may be impeached."

We have heard time and time again that the evidence reflects the payment to defendants [of] money. The President had knowledge that these funds were being paid and these were funds collected for the 1972 presidential campaign. We know that the President met with Mr. Henry Petersen twenty-seven times to discuss matters related to Watergate, and immediately thereafter met with the very persons who were implicated in the information Mr. Petersen was receiving. The words are: "If the President is connected in any suspicious manner with any person and there be grounds to believe that he will shelter that person, he may be impeached."

Justice Story: "Impeachment" is attended—"is intended for occasional and extraordinary cases where a superior power acting for the whole people is put into operation to protect their rights and rescue their liberties from violations." We know about the Huston plan. We know about the break-in of the psychiatrist's office. We know that there was absolute complete direction on September 3rd when the President indicated that a surreptitious entry had been made in Dr. Fielding's office, after having met with Mr. Ehrlichman and Mr. Young. "Protect their rights." "Rescue their liberties from violation."

The Carolina ratification convention impeachment criteria: those are impeachable "who behave amiss or betray their public trust." Beginning shortly after the Watergate break-in and continuing to the present time, the President has engaged in a series of public statements and actions designed to thwart the lawful investigation by government prosecutors. Moreover, the President has made public announcements and assertions bearing on the Watergate case, which the evidence will show he knew to be false. These assertions, false assertions, impeachable, those who misbehave. Those who "behave amiss or betray the public trust."

James Madison again at the Constitutional Convention: "A President is impeachable if he attempts to subvert the Constitution." The Constitution charges the President with the task of taking care that the laws be faithfully executed, and yet the President has counseled his aides to commit perjury, willfully disregard the secrecy of grand jury proceedings, conceal surreptitious entry, attempt to compromise a federal judge, while publicly displaying his cooperation with the processes of criminal justice. "A President is impeachable if he attempts to subvert the Constitution."

If the impeachment provision in the Constitution of the United States will not reach the offenses charged here, then perhaps that eighteenth-century Constitution should be abandoned to a twentieth-century paper shredder.

Has the President committed offenses, and planned, and directed, and acquiesced in a course of conduct which the Constitution will not tolerate? That's the question. We know that. We know the question. We should now forthwith proceed to answer the question. It is reason, and not passion, which must guide our deliberations, guide our debate, and guide our decision.

I yield back the balance of my time, Mr. Chairman.

Mary Fisher's 1992 Republican National Convention Address

August 19, 1992
Houston, Texas

Less than three months ago at platform hearings in Salt Lake City, I asked the Republican Party to lift the shroud of silence which has been draped over the issue of HIV and AIDS. I have come tonight to bring our silence to an end. I bear a message of challenge, not self-congratulation. I want your attention, not your applause.

I would never have asked to be HIV positive, but I believe that in all things there is a purpose; and I stand before you and before the nation gladly. The reality of AIDS is brutally clear. Two hundred thousand Americans are dead or dying. A million more are infected. Worldwide, forty million, sixty million, or a hundred million infections will be counted in the coming few years. But despite science and research, White House meetings, and congressional hearings, despite good intentions and bold initiatives, campaign slogans, and hopeful promises, it is—despite it all—the epidemic which is winning tonight.

In the context of an election year, I ask you, here in this great hall, or listening in the quiet of your home, to recognize that AIDS virus is not a political creature. It does not care whether you are Democrat or Republican; it does not ask whether you are black or white, male or female, gay or straight, young or old.

Tonight, I represent an AIDS community whose members have been reluctantly drafted from every segment of American society. Though I am white and a mother, I am one with a black infant struggling with tubes in a Philadelphia hospital. Though I am female and contracted this disease in marriage and enjoy the warm support of my family, I am one with the lonely gay man sheltering a flickering candle from the cold wind of his family's rejection.

This is not a distant threat. It is a present danger. The rate of infection is increasing fastest among women and children. Largely unknown a decade ago, AIDS is the third leading killer of young adult Americans today. But it won't be third for long, because unlike other diseases, this one travels. Adolescents don't give each other cancer or heart disease because they believe they are in love, but HIV is different; and we have helped it along. We have killed each other with our ignorance, our prejudice, and our silence.

We may take refuge in our stereotypes, but we cannot hide there long, because HIV asks only one thing of those it attacks. Are you human? And this is the right question. Are you human? Because people with HIV have not entered some alien state of being. They are human. They have not earned cruelty, and they do not deserve meanness. They don't benefit from being isolated or treated as outcasts. Each of them is exactly what God made: a person; not evil, deserving of our judgment; not victims, longing for our pity—people, ready for support and worthy of compassion.

My call to you, my Party, is to take a public stand, no less compassionate than that of the President and Mrs. Bush. They have embraced me and my family in memorable ways. In the place of judgment, they have shown affection. In difficult moments, they have raised our spirits. In the darkest hours, I have seen them reaching not only to me, but also to my parents, armed with that stunning grief and special grace that comes only to parents who have themselves leaned too long over the bedside of a dying child.

With the President's leadership, much good has been done. Much of the good has gone unheralded, and as the President has insisted, much remains to be done. But we do the President's cause no good if we praise the American family but ignore a virus that destroys it.

We must be consistent if we are to be believed. We cannot love justice and ignore prejudice, love our children and fear to teach them. Whatever our role as parent or policymaker, we must act as eloquently as we speak—else we have no integrity. My call to the nation is a plea for awareness. If you believe you are safe, you are in danger. Because I was not hemophiliac, I was not at risk. Because I was not gay, I was not at risk. Because I did not inject drugs, I was not at risk.

My father has devoted much of his lifetime guarding against another Holocaust. He is part of the generation who heard Pastor Nemoellor come out of the Nazi death camps to say, "They came after the Jews, and I was not a Jew, so, I did not protest. They came after the trade unionists, and I was not a trade unionist, so, I did not protest. Then they came after the Roman Catholics, and I was not a Roman Catholic, so, I did not protest. Then they came after me, and there was no one left to protest."

The—the lesson history teaches is this: If you believe you are safe, you are at risk. If you do not see this killer stalking your children, look again. There is no family or community, no race or religion, no place left in America that is safe. Until we genuinely embrace this message, we are a nation at risk.

Tonight, HIV marches resolutely toward AIDS in more than a million American homes, littering its pathway with the bodies of the young—young men, young women, young parents, and young children. One of the families is mine. If it is true that HIV inevitably turns to AIDS, then my children will inevitably turn to orphans. My family has been a rock of support.

My eighty-four-year-old father, who has pursued the healing of the nations, will not accept the premise that he cannot heal his daughter. My mother refuses to be broken. She still calls at midnight to tell wonderful jokes that make me laugh. Sisters and friends, and my brother Phillip, whose birthday is today, all have helped carry me over the hardest places. I am blessed, richly and deeply blessed, to have such a family.

But not all of you—but not all of you have been so blessed. You are HIV positive, but dare not say it. You have lost loved ones, but you dare not whisper the word AIDS. You weep silently. You grieve alone. I have a message for you. It is not you who should feel shame. It is we—we who tolerate ignorance and practice prejudice, we who have taught you to fear. We must lift our shroud of silence, making it safe for you to reach out for compassion. It is our task to seek safety for our children, not in quiet denial, but in effective action.

Someday our children will be grown. My son Max, now four, will take the measure of his mother. My son Zachary, now two, will sort through his memories. I may not be here to hear their judgments, but I know already what I hope they are. I want my children to know that their mother was not a victim. She was a messenger. I do not want them to think, as I once did, that courage is the absence of fear. I want them to know that courage is the strength to act wisely when most we are afraid. I want them to have the courage to step forward when called by their nation or their Party and give leadership, no matter what the personal cost.

I ask no more of you than I ask of myself or of my children. To the millions of you who are grieving, who are frightened, who have suffered the ravages of AIDS first-hand: Have courage, and you will find support. To the millions who are strong, I issue the plea: Set aside prejudice and politics to make room for compassion and sound policy.

To my children, I make this pledge: I will not give in, Zachary, because I draw my courage from you. Your silly giggle gives me hope; your gentle prayers give me strength; and you, my child, give me the reason to say to America, "You are at risk." And I will not rest, Max, until I have done all I can to make your world safe. I will seek a place where intimacy is not the prelude to suffering. I will not hurry to leave you, my children, but when I go, I pray that you will not suffer shame on my account.

To all within the sound of my voice, I appeal: Learn with me the lessons of history and of grace, so my children will not be afraid to say the word "AIDS" when I am gone. Then, their children and yours may not need to whisper it at all.

God bless the children, and God bless us all.

Good night.

Glossary

alliteration: A figure of emphasis that occurs through the repetition of initial consonant letters (or sounds) in two or more different words across successive sentences, clauses, or phrases.

allusion: A figure of amplification that connects a present moment in a speech to some notable and typically well-known person, place, thing, event, or statement situated in the past.

anaphora: A figure of emphasis in which the first word or set of words is repeated across successive phrases or clauses. Example: "We are a people in a quandary about the present. We are a people in search of our future. We are a people in search of a national community."

antimetabole: A figure of balance where the order of words are reversed across successive clauses and phrases. Example: "Mankind must put an end to war or war will put an end to mankind."

antithesis: A figure of balance that presents two contrasting or opposing ideas in adjacent phrases, clauses, or sentences. Example: "We find ourselves rich in goods but ragged in spirit, reaching with magnificent precision for the moon but falling into raucous discord on earth."

argument: A debatable proposition supported by at least one other proposition.

chronological: A temporal pattern of arrangement in which the main ideas of a speech are advanced sequentially as they naturally do or might occur in time.

conclusion: The final section in the macrostructure of a speech, the content of which provides rational and psychological closure from the content preceding it.

content: That body of ideas and arguments transmitted by a speaker to produce rational and emotional effects on an audience.

cultural maxim: A statement that conveys a general or probable truth intrinsic to a given culture or subculture.

delivery: The verbal and nonverbal means by which content is transmitted between speaker and audience.

ethos: One of three Aristotelian modes of persuasion, referring to a speaker's credibility as perceived by an audience. Aristotle noted that ethos takes several forms, including moral virtue or character, practical wisdom, and goodwill.

extemporaneous: A type of delivery that is based on a working familiarity with the speech but that relies on an outline or set of notes.

impromptu: A type of delivery where a speaker has done very little to no preparation for a particular speech and uses very few, if any, notes.

logos: One of three Aristotelian modes of persuasion, referring to the mix of main and supporting propositions that together constitute arguments calculated to win the rational assent of an audience.

master metaphor: A core or grounding comparison between two different things from which the content of an entire speech gets its particular interpretive slant.

metaphor: A figure of explication occurring when a comparison is made by speaking of one thing in terms of another; an implied comparison between two *different* things that share at least one attribute in common; an association between two unlike things (A vs. B) achieved by borrowing the language that refers to thing A and applying it to thing B. (Not to be confused with **simile**.) Example: "Why this country is a shining city on a hill."

narrative: A persuasive strategy employing a coherent and compelling story formed from a strategic selection of relevant facts, characters, and events usually arranged chronologically.

narrative frame: The "lenses" through which we make sense of a narrative; a perspective through which we interpret the meaning of a given narrative.

parallelism: A syntactically balanced string of phrases or clauses. Example: "We have seen the state of our Union in the endurance of rescuers working past exhaustion. We've seen the unfurling of flags, the lighting of candles, the giving of blood, the saying of prayers—in English, Hebrew, and Arabic."

pathos: One of three Aristotelian modes of persuasion, referring to the use of content to induce particular emotions in an audience.

problem-solution: A type of progression format that allows for a discussion of problems and their significance, a detailed explication of the plausible solutions, a consideration of alternative solutions, and an assessment of the new problems that will accrue if a given solution is taken.

purpose: The general aim of a speech; general purposes include to educate, to persuade, to entertain, and to console; in the realm of persuasive speaking, a rhetorical purpose targets two main objectives: human belief and human action. Speeches attempt to create, influence, reinforce, undermine, and even destroy beliefs. In addition, public speeches may also motivate us to take or to refrain from taking some action.

rapport: A state of mutual identification between speaker and audience.

rhetoric: A persuasive, purpose-driven public communication containing content, structure, style, and delivery that emanates from a rhetorical situation.

rhetorical situation: A context in which a problem or crisis is capable of being redressed in whole or in part through the power of speech alone. Features includes a problem or crisis, a purpose, an audience, a subject, and, of course, a speaker.

simile: A figure of explication in which two things that share at least one attribute are explicitly associated with each other; an overt comparison between two unlike things as though they were similar—usually with the words *like* or *as*. Example: "A Republic whose history, like the path of the just, is as the shining light that shineth more and more unto the perfect day."

structural motif: A recurring phrase or word that captures the central theme of a speech.

structure: The macrostructure of a speech concerning the large-scale division of content into three general parts: introduction, body, and conclusion. The microstructure of a speech concerns the division of these three general parts into smaller units or subsections.

style: The kind and level of language and associated linguistic devices used to convey content in view of a given rhetorical situation.

topical: A structural pattern in which main ideas are divided and arranged by type, kind, genus, and so on.

triplicate asyndeton: A figure of expression in which three words with the same or close to the same number of syllables are set off by omitting a normally occurring conjunction. Example: "I came, I saw, I conquered" or "Duty, honor, country."

References

Aghahowa, B. E. "Grace Under Fire: The Rhetoric of Watergate and Patriotism, Barbara Jordan Style." Doctoral dissertation, University of Illinois at Chicago, January 2005.

Aristotle, and George A. Kennedy. *On Rhetoric: A Theory of Civic Discourse.* (2nd ed.) New York: Oxford University Press, 2007.

Bebbington, David. "Evangelicalism in Its Settings: The British and American Movements Since 1940." In *Evangelicalism*, edited by Mark A. Noll, David W. Bebbington, and George A. Rawlyk, 365–388. New York: Oxford University Press, 1994.

Bitzer, Lloyd. 1968. "The Rhetorical Situation." *Rhetoric and Philosophy*, 1: 1–14.

Bly, Nellie. *The Kennedy Men: Three Generations of Sex, Scandal, and Secrets.* New York: Kensington Books, 1996.

Bohlen, Celestine. "Kennedy Visits the Falwell Empire; Liberal Force Meets Conservative Boston." *Washington Post*, October 4, 1983, A1.

Branham, R. J., and Pearce, W. B. 1987. "A Contract for Civility: Edward Kennedy's Lynchburg Address." *Quarterly Journal of Speech*, 73, 424–443.

Burgchardt, Carl. "Barbara Charline Jordan (1936–1996), Lawyer, U.S. Representative, Professor." In *African-American Orators: A Bio-Critical Sourcebook*, edited by Richard W. Leeman, 207–217. Westport, CT: Greenwood Press, 1996.

Clarke, Thurston. *Ask Not*. New York: Henry Holt & Company, 2004.

Clymer, Adam. *Edward M. Kennedy: A Biography*. New York: William Morrow & Company, 1999.

Eddings, Jerelyn. "The Voice of Eloquent Thunder." *U.S. News & World Report* 120, no. 4 (January 29, 1996): 16.

Falwell, Jerry. *Strength for the Journey: An Autobiography*. New York: Simon and Schuster, 1987.

Fisher, Mary. *My Name Is Mary*. New York: Scribner, 1996.

Gailey, Phil. "Kennedy Tells Falwell Group of Tolerance." *New York Times*, October 3, 1983, E4.

Hatch, Nathan O. *The Democratization of American Christianity*. New Haven: Yale University Press, 1989.

Johnstone, Barbara. *The Linguistic Individual: Self-Expression in Language and Linguistics*. New York: Oxford University Press, 1996.

Jordan, Barbara, and Shelby Hearon. *Barbara Jordan: A Self-Portrait*. Garden City, NY: Doubleday, 1979.

MacArthur, Douglas. *Reminiscences: General of the Army*. New York: McGraw-Hill, 1964.

Manchester, William. *American Caesar: Douglas MacArthur 1880–1964*. Boston: Little, Brown, 1978.

Mendelsohn, James. *Barbara Jordan: Getting Things Done*. Brookfield, CT: Twenty-First Century Books, 2000.

Mister, Steven M. 1986. "Reagan's *Challenger* Tribute: Combining Generic Constraints and Situational Demands." *Central States Speech Journal*, 37(3), 158–165.

Muir, William L. "Ronald Reagan's Bully Pulpit: Creating a Rhetoric of Values." In *Presidential Speechwriting: From the New Deal to the Reagan Revolution and Beyond*, edited by Kurt Ritter and Martin J. Medhurst, 195–216. College Station, TX: Texas A&M University Press, 2003.

Perret, Geoffrey. *Old Soldiers Never Die: The Life of Douglas MacArthur*. New York: Random House, 1996.

Rogers, Mary Beth. 1999. "The School Years of Barbara Jordan." *The Journal of Blacks in Higher Education*, 23, 116–122.

Scott, Norman, Jr. 1999. "MacArthur's Last Battle." *American Heritage*, 50, no. 8, 20–22.

Thomas, Cal. "The Man Who Came to Dinner." *Washington Post*, October 9, 1983, C7.

Witner, Lawrence S., ed. *MacArthur*. Englewood Cliffs, NJ: Prentice Hall, 1971.

Woodward, Gary C. *Persuasive Encounters: Case Studies in Constructive Confrontation*. New York: Praeger Publishers, 1990.

About the Author

MICHAEL E. EIDENMULLER, Ph.D. (Louisiana State University), was born in San Francisco and raised in Orange County, California. He currently resides in Whitehouse, Texas, where he is a professor of speech communication at the University of Texas at Tyler. He is the creator and owner of AmericanRhetoric.com, *American Rhetoric: The Power of Oratory in the United States*, the Internet's premiere online library of freely available American political, social movement, religious, and movie speeches delivered during the past seventy years in text, audio, and video formats. The site attracts some 500 thousand visitors per month in nearly 200 countries and has been featured in the *Christian Science Monitor, The Hollywood Reporter, PC Magazine, BBC World*, and the *Voice of America*, among others.